THE BUSINESS OF A SUCCESSFUL MARRIAGE

Treating Your Marriage Like a Business

by

Sheila D Green

Copyright © 2019 Sheila D Green

All rights reserved.

All rights reserved. No portion of the book may be reproduced or utilized in any form or by any means, electronic or mechanical, including photocopying, recording, or by any other information storage and retrieval system, without permission in writing from the author.

ISBN print: 978-1-7343980-0-7

ISBN mobi: 978-1-7343980-1-4

ISBN ePUB: 978-1-7343980-2-1

Dedication

I would like to dedicate this book to Lee, my husband of 32 years. I am blessed to have him by my side.

To my children, Kamaria and Lee III who are our gifts from God.

Table of Contents

Dedication 3

Acknowledgment 7

Preface 9

Introduction 13

PRINCIPLE #1 Marriage-Business Plan 21
    Planning a successful marriage 22

PRINCIPLE #2 Know the Mission 31
    Clarifying your expectations 37
    Monogamy and Marriage 39

PRINCIPLE #3 Know Your Customer/ Know Your Spouse 45

PRINCIPLE #4 Great Communication Is Key 55
    Negative nonverbal communication 59
    Agree to Disagree 60
    Forgive and forget 62
    Using economic approaches to managing conflicts in marriage 63
    Benefits of an active listener 66
    Business Language and Love Language 67

Characteristics of Love Languages 70
Talking straight in your relationship 71
Demonstrating Respect in Relationships 72

PRINCIPLE #5 Time Management 75
Time Management 79
Date Night 84
Keep learning 85

PRINCIPLE #6 Providing Safety and Security 87

PRINCIPLE #7 Having a Solid Financial Plan 93
Financial management 98
Joint or separate accounts? 101

PRINCIPLE #8 Keeping Health and Wellness as High Priorities . 103

PRINCIPLE #9 Evaluate and Then Evaluate Again 109
Conducting a SWOT Analysis 114
It can only get better 117

PRINCIPLE #10 Understanding and Living Our Culture and Values 119
Unconditional Love 121
Faithfulness 122
Peace 124
Forgiveness 126
Intimacy 127
Unity 128

PRINCIPLE #11 No Business Allowed 131

CONCLUSION 137

Acknowledgment

I want to thank God, for without Him nothing is possible.

To my husband Lee, who has always seen my value and pushed me past my comfort zone.

To my daughter Kamaria who has shown me that struggles are like hurdles, they require you to move upward and over...she soars.

To my son Lee who has confirmed that growth is like an artist's canvas; each stroke is your individual mark toward your purpose and destiny.

To my grandmother; Mary Johnson (who has gone on to be with Lord) for all the "nuggets" of wisdom that have guided me on my journey.

To a host of family and friends who have had a major impact upon my life.

Preface

If you have ever been married, you know that marriage is all about compromise. You make compromises on who will do the dishes, who will take out the trash, who will change the next dirty diaper, who will walk the dog, and so on and so forth. These issues seem unique to marriage, but marital unions actually have a lot in common with businesses. If you're going to have a successful business, you have to make compromises as well. Managing a marriage is just like managing a business. You have to plan, delegate, motivate, strategize, pivot, inspire, mediate, grow, budget and reward.

Marriage is essentially a business merger and runs smoothly when both businesses in the merger clearly understand the terms. The best part about treating your marriage like a business is that you enter the relationship knowing that you want to build something together that will be solid, strong and successful. Businesses that are successful are built upon values that all leaders and team members share.

Those of you who own businesses or work as part of a larger corporation respect your job, respect your co-workers, respect your boss and respect your paycheck! Without this respect, you set yourself, and everyone around you up for failure. And lots of businesses fail – *Forbes* reports that 8 out of every 10 new businesses fail in the first 18 months! These businesses fail because they don't understand their customers, lack clear values, have poor leadership, and can't get a grip on their finances. In short, a lot of factors can sink a new business quickly and the same is true for a marriage.

You and your spouse need to understand the customer – in this case – each other. You can't successfully provide what the other needs if you don't take time to find out. You both need to identify and hold each other accountable to clearly outlined values, as these will guide your decisions. You also need strong leadership – logical choices that align with your values that prioritize the health of the marriage. And, you have to manage your finances. A lack of cash flow and poor money management can cause stress and conflict which ultimately causes you to lose the very things your marriage needs for safety and security.

In other words, you prioritize your job or your business and you should prioritize your marriage the same way. You respect the work that you do and that's why you do it so well. You respect the company's standards and processes, and you respect the returns that result from following those standards and processes. You show up every day ready to work with an understanding of what's expected of you and what it takes to get results.

Though it's not always easy, you know you should approach each day with an optimistic attitude and be willing to compromise and negotiate in order to run a successful business. Your marriage requires the same level of dedication and awareness. You don't clock in or out at home, because you're always on the clock and with that comes a series of expectations that, if not followed, could put your marriage in jeopardy.

Treat your marriage like a business, and your marriage will enjoy all kinds of bonuses, benefits, and rewards.

Introduction

Individuals who have owned a business or worked in the business world understand what it takes to be successful. There are certain principles and steps that are required to ensure that the business is thriving. Many individuals are taking critical steps that they know will help make their business successful and the same holds true for their marriage. We need to start thinking about our marriage like a business. Just as we all have thoughts on how to keep our business productive, we need to think about our marriages in this manner.

In most business situations, individuals plan for success and they strongly believe that success can be achieved. They picture their business as a success and do whatever it takes to ensure that happens. There are so many marriages that are struggling and many have ended up in divorce. One of the reasons why marriages are not successful is that we do not put the same time and effort into the marriage as we put into our business or our jobs.

We know what it takes to make sure our business is a success and we take the necessary steps for that success; but many married couples fail to do the same thing for their marriages. In business, we make sure we put in the necessary time and energy but in our marriage, we often don't invest the time. In business, we implement strategies to ensure financial success but in our marriage, we don't pay close attention to money. In business, we make sure we have a business plan but in our marriage we tend not to have a plan. In business, we ensure that the employees take time off to recharge. In marriages, we typically do not take needed vacations and spend quality time together. By now, I think you get the point. We must start thinking about marriage as a business and only then can we expect the rewards, just as we are rewarded handsomely when our businesses are successful.

The first critical step is to have an overall plan for the marriage. This is the very first thing you do with a business. You take time and effort to put together a plan of action. You have to know what the plan is and where you want to go with the business – the same is true with your marriage.

There are 11 key areas that we will focus on that are taken from critical business principles. These areas include: starting with a strategic plan, knowing the mission, knowing your business and your business partner, understanding the importance of communication, utilizing time management principles, understanding the importance of safety and security, having a solid financial plan, prioritizing health and wellness, understanding the importance of evaluating the situation, understanding and embracing the culture of the business (spirituality) and, lastly, a section that is more intimate where there is no business allowed.

In this book, I'll be discussing 11 business principles that should be considered to help build a successful marriage. These principles are what make any business successful and can also make your marriage successful. Here's a quick summary of each principle;

Principle #1: If you think about it carefully, every business starts off with a business plan. I cannot think of any successful business that has ever been created that started off without having a well thought out plan of what they wanted to accomplish, how they would go about accomplishing it, what money would be needed, and having an understanding of the customer. I would venture to say that our marriages are more important than our businesses, however, we do not put the same thought into the plans for our marriage. We just hope and pray that things will work out for our good. I believe that couples need to put in the same time planning their marriage that business owners put in for planning their successful business. This is the first basic step in building a great marriage.

Principle #2: It is absolutely critical for any business to know and understand its mission, vision, and strategic direction and that applies to marriage. Many couples go into a marriage with no real plan or sense of direction. You might ask, how is it that couples may not be heading in the same direction? Many think that a successful marriage involves just staying married or surviving, but it's actually about a journey that should be productive and rewarding. This can only happen when couples understand the mission and vision for their marriage.

Principle #3: It is also important for the business owner to completely understand the business they are in and the customers they are trying to reach. This involves research and a lot of groundwork so that they are clear about what it will take to be successful in that area. We know that if you don't study and clearly understand what you are getting into, the business would most likely fail; this is also true for marriages.

It is also important to know your business partners and employees. Knowing and learning the people that you are involved with will be helpful to your success. This includes knowing what makes them tick, how to get the most out of them, what rewards they like, and what their strengths and weaknesses are. By understanding your business partners, you can prevent situations that would result in conflicts and that's how a marriage should operate. If you really know your spouse's strengths, weaknesses, likes, and dislikes, you can create opportunities for greater success.

Principle #4: Communication is key! We have heard this on numerous occasions and I believe it is the bedrock of a successful business and marriage. Everything falls apart when communication isn't clear and direct and that would surely lead to failure. This will be one of the most important business principles that should be applied to having a successful marriage as most of the principles of success revolve around good communication.

Principle #5: Time management for businesses is also vital as it is important to utilize your time for development and growth. If you are not managing your time wisely, your business will fail – it's that simple. This is why many businesses perform what is called a "time study." A time study reveals how you are spending your time and how productive you have been. How are you spending your time with your spouse? Are you spending time together or are you spending time on social media? It is not just about spending time together but ensuring that you're spending quality time together. Couples must get intentional about making time for each other.

Another time management strategy businesses utilize is putting things on a calendar. It may seem unusual for married couples to schedule time on a calendar to be together, but it works. There is a saying that I heard recently that I believe is so true - "the things that are written down are the things that get done." So scheduling time on a calendar to spend time together as a couple is a good strategy.

Principle #6: The safety and security of a marriage cannot be taken for granted. In business, the owners make sure that they put safeguards in place to ensure that the business and all of the assets are safe and secure. They provide security for employees so that they feel good about their position and marriage should operate under the same principle. Both individuals in the marriage need to feel that sense of safety and security. The wife knows that her man has her back and they have nothing to worry about and the husband understands that he has a safe and secure place with his woman; he can share all of his intimate thoughts, feelings, and insecurities.

Principle #7: The core of any business are the finances and that's why a business starts by drafting out a financial plan. They have to understand what it will take to run the business and the expected financial returns. Without a financial plan, the business will have no clue in terms of the income that can be generated and if the expenses will outweigh the expected income. With marriages, most couples don't even think about the financial aspect. They go to work to get a paycheck with no overall plan for income, budgets and other financial matters that are important. One of the first things that married couples need to do is have a discussion about finances and make sure that they are on the same page. It has been well documented that money issues is one of the top reasons that marriages end in divorce.

Principle #8: Most companies want to ensure that their employees are healthy. So, they provide opportunities for their employees to participate in health and wellness plans. They also provide resources to help their employees maintain a healthy mind and body. In a marriage, it is also critical for the couple to pinpoint health and wellness as one of the main priorities. They must support each other in eating right, exercising, and monitoring alcohol and drug intake. They should encourage each other to get regular check-ups. An important aspect of being healthy is taking time off. In business, you get paid time off, commonly referred to as PTO. The married couple also needs to ensure that they take time off and take periodic vacations. Just like employees need time to rest and recharge, the same holds true for married couples.

Principle #9: A part of any business is to take a look at what is working and what is not. In other words, this means evaluating the business or evaluating the marriage. Evaluation is a critical step in any business. It is also critical in a marriage. You must be able to examine what is going well and what needs work. You must be able to take an honest look at the successes and failures. What parts are weak and what parts are strong? If you evaluate and determine what is happening, you can then put a plan in place to make adjustments to fix the issues and continue to implement what is successful. Many married couples never step back and do an overall assessment or evaluation of their marriage. They just continue to do business or marriage as usual.

Principle #10: Most businesses or companies have what they consider a "culture" of the organization. The culture might include things like respect and dignity. The culture would be those values that everyone in the organization shares. It is the overall theme of what holds each other and the business together. These are behaviors, beliefs, and experiences that we all share as co-workers. Like businesses, each marriage will also have a culture.

In this book, I will look at spirituality as the culture of the marriage. For those who do not believe in God, this culture may not work for you. However, there will be cultural norms that your marriage will need to focus on. I believe that God and your spirituality should be the nucleus of your marriage. Having God as the center provides that culture that will drive everything else towards success. Couples should pray together, attend church together, study God's word together and do different ministries together. It will be crucial for you to establish that marital culture around your relationship with God.

Principle #11: In most businesses and organizations, employees try to set aside that time when they take off from work and enjoy themselves. In some cases, they call this "happy hour," where employees can go out, have fun and not talk about work. The same holds true for marriage. This principle in marriage, however, will focus on intimacy.

There should be those times when there is no business allowed and nothing happens but intimacy- that important period when the couple only focuses on each other. This is where sexual intimacy comes into play. Having a plan in place to ensure that you are spending that "happy hour" or intentional time together is critical. I call this "no business allowed." This may also require that you make your bedroom free of anything related to business or work. There may be a recommendation to not have your cell phone in the bedroom, no TV, no office, no computer, or any other devices. Your bedroom should be a place where you can retreat, and just focus on intimacy. The intimacy is that part that really creates the unmistakable bond between you and your spouse.

There are so many other business principles that can be included in this list. However, these are the ones that I feel are most critical for the success of the marriage. If you start with these 11 principles, I believe you will be on your way to a marriage that will be named as one of the Fortune 100 marriages in the world.

PRINCIPLE #1

Marriage-Business Plan

Just like in business, marriage is built on the basis of partnership and this partnership is usually intended for a lifetime. Business owners always envision partnerships with someone who has the same priorities, values, dreams, and ambitions. They tend to have preconceived expectations from their business partners even before the establishment of the business and without proper planning and strategizing. This is also true in a marriage where one partner has already mapped out plans of what marriage should look like without the inclusion of the other partner. No marriage has ever worked out with the expectations and arrangements of just one partner. Every marriage needs a plan that should involve both partners.

Planning a Successful Marriage

I like to believe that marriages are made in heaven, after all, marriage is a covenant. However, marriage plans and the expectations that come with it have to be made on earth.

Do not forget, wedding plans are not marriage plans. Most couples work tirelessly towards planning a successful wedding. Couples give their all to make sure everything aligns with their dream wedding.

Do not get me wrong! Planning a wedding is absolutely necessary. Plus most everyone, particularly women, loves a fairytale wedding. However, if a couple invests the time used in planning their wedding into planning their marriage, they would have a great start and a strong foundation for their marriage. You should understand that planning the marriage is much more important than just planning the wedding event.

A wedding is a one day event that only takes a few hours, that involves lots of family, friends, and acquaintances. A marriage, on the other hand, is a union that requires more than a few hours. It is the journey of a lifetime that involves just you and your partner. All of your family and friends return to their various ways of life after the wedding, but both of you begin your life of living together. So, between the planning of the wedding and the planning of the marriage, which do you think is more important? No business partner starts a business without first strategizing and analyzing ideas and long term plans. Marriage, work schedules, investments, and family planning should be discussed before the wedding. Do not happily say 'I Do' today and become confused about what to do tomorrow.

So what are the 'strategic plans' for a successful marriage?

Ask questions:

Most people find it awkward to ask their potential partner basic questions. Even asking 'what do you do for a living' is now seen as derogatory when in fact, that is a basic question anyone should ask early in the relationship. There are other questions that should be asked during the period of courtship and before the 'wedding bells.'

Basically, these questions are divided into two sections. The first section includes the questions you should ask yourself. They are:

- Why do I want to get married?
- Why should it be this person?
- How well do I know my potential partner?
- What are their strengths and weaknesses?

- How important is money to you?
- Do I have a clear understanding of my feelings and expectations?
- What do I value most in a partner?

Note that these questions are for you to consider.. Also, while answering these questions, be sure to be realistic and not superficial. Be reasonable enough and never concede to putting off important points just for the sake of wanting to get married.

The second section consists of questions for both partners;

- Where do you want to live after the wedding?
- Do you want kids? If yes, how many?
- How long would you want to wait before having kids?
- Who would watch over the kids? Will either of you stay home while the other works or would you consider external childcare?
- How do you plan budgets for the family?
- Should we use a joint bank account or separate bank accounts?
- How do we divide the household chores?
- What are your financial goals?
- What are your views on having a close friendship with the opposite-sex?
- What are your boundaries when it comes to sex?

This list of questions is not exhaustive for both sections, however, these questions may spark conversations that will have to be addressed in order to have a successful marriage.

Know thyself:

No one should ever go into a business without first knowing how to deal with situations of loss, disagreements and disappointments. You must be fully aware of who you are before going into partnership with someone else. Know your weaknesses and your strengths. How will you react to situations such as financial crises, addictions, and infidelity? Make a checklist and identify your fears and insecurities and make efforts to become the best partner you can possibly be.

Do not ignore the red flags:

This is an essential aspect that most potential partners neglect with the intent of "I will change her" or "He will change over time." but it is better to identify these 'red flags' before you get married. These red flags are not just some flaws you could possibly live with, there are traits that you won't condone or make excuses for. Problems in many marriages set in when red flags are neglected. A nagging wife was also a nagging girlfriend but maybe you chose to chalk it up because she cooks well. That jealous husband was also a jealous boyfriend but you ignored the signs because he was the cutest guy you've ever dated. Identify what those red flags are and do not accept the mindset that your partner will change for you.

Be clear about your expectations:

Having unrealistic expectations can possibly create a strain on the relationship when eventually the other partner does not measure up to the standard. This is not saying you should lower your standards. You should understand that we all have our flaws and you make the choice of those you can live with.

Evaluate your financial goals:

Before any business partnership takes place, the two partners must have assessed their available finances and decide how much should go into the business. It is very essential to discuss your plans for financial matters with your partner. Do not assume either of you know what to do when it comes to providing, spending and making money. Discuss the expenses, income and savings with your partner so you are on the same page regarding your finances. Both of you should be aware of where the money goes and where it is being kept; ensure you both are part of making all financial decisions.

Make a decision to talk about everything:

Before saying "I DO", you must agree to be open to communication with your partner. Agree to talk about anything and everything to avoid stifling your relationship with your partner and creating a destructive distance.

Household chores:

This is seemingly a frustrating situation that can be easily solved. Usually only one partner takes care of the household chores and this can cause tension. The partner who is doing all the work becomes resentful and complains about running the activities of the house alone. In a bid to avoid major conflicts arising from an issue as trivial as household chores, both partners should sit down and discuss who should handle a particular chore. You live in the house together so why not handle your household chores equally.

Attend marriage seminars:

Do not wait until there are problems in your marriage before you seek counseling. Search for christian counselors or authentic and unbiased marriage counseling centers. It is about investing in your marriage from the very beginning. Marriage classes can bring about growth and good innovations to your marriage; you can meet older experienced couples that can give good advice on how to improve your relationship. This would boost your relationship and strengthen your bond.

Read books on maintaining a healthy marriage:

An entrepreneur with a vision to succeed should have read lots of books and attended business seminars before embarking on any business pursuit. The same holds true for marriage. Good marriage practices can be obtained from reading books and attending marriage seminars. Many books will provide workbooks that encourage you to do the exercises together and discuss ideas to put into practice.

Setting marriage goals:

The first three months of your marriage can be incredibly thrilling - you are still basking in the euphoria of your honeymoon, but, do you have any marriage goals in place yet? A year or so after your wedding will become a reality check if you do not have goals or visions in place for your marriage. Even if you failed to set goals before saying "I DO", you can still do it now. Start setting goals- it is your marriage, own it and start planning for it properly. Marriage should be a marathon and not a sprint, marathons always need proper planning and constant re-evaluation.

Proper planning and constant reevaluation includes:

Communication goals:

This should be the main goal of every couple; talking about anything and everything with your partner. Communication should also include listening to what your partner has to say on any issue. Most times, our focus is mainly on talking to our partner without listening, which could lead to serious disagreement and conflicts. Focus on having a great conversation with your partner while being attentive, slow to speak, and slow to anger. This kind of goal will lead to less arguments and more improvements in your relationship.

Companionship and intimacy goals:

People have various reasons for getting married. Some to keep up with the demands of society, while for others the aim is to have children. In the midst of fulfilling our various reasons, we forget the basis of all relationships, which is companionship. Companionship and intimacy are critically important for any successful relationship. It is having that special kind of intimacy with that one person you love. When we do not focus on setting intimacy goals, separation begins to surround our thoughts, we begin to see no reason why you should remain with our partner. Be serious about setting intimacy goals, it could be date nights, time alone at home, vacations, attending concerts together, etc. Find possible ways out of your busy schedule and create quality time with each other. Stay close and focused on having a healthy intimate relationship.

Sex goals:

Married couples tend to shy away from this particular topic. This is a pivotal aspect of the life of every couple. Sex keeps the marriage alive and active. The goal should be satisfying each other sexually; find out your partner's likes and dislikes and explore these areas together. Understand what tickles their sexual fancy and work on them. Talk about it and focus on getting better.

Forgiveness goals:

I always like to refer to this part as the 'deal breaker goals.' What are the things either of you can not live without? What are the things that could keep you resentful forever? What is your deal breaker? What are those things that your partner would do that you will not condone? Either you or your partner are going to make mistakes. So it is important to set goals on dealing with imperfections and misunderstandings because they are bound to happen. Talk about these things and acknowledge the fact that you are also imperfect. This acknowledgment of your imperfection will help you in the area of forgiveness.

Spiritual goals:

"We are too busy for prayers," "we pray individually, we don't have time for couple's prayers." These are just a few examples of excuses given by most couples for not finding the time to pray together. When we set spiritual goals – setting aside time for prayer and ministry, then nothing would become an obstacle to our prayer lives. Praying together as a couple is an amazing advantage many married couples do not know about.

Have you ever heard the saying "the couple that prays together stays together?" Prayers said in pure, genuine love and unity of spirit are always powerful, and these should be the traits of every couple - pure genuine love and unity.

It does not necessarily have to be a large undertaking, it could be a simple searching for souls while meeting a particular need in your community together. Both partners can start out with volunteering, teaching Bible principles, or teaching in the youth church, in order to reach more people. The beautiful thing about working in a ministry is that it strengthens your spiritual life and tightens your bond as a couple.

Charity goals:

Maybe either partner is charitable and could give out anything they possess but now that you are married or intending to get married, decisions should be made about charity together. Set goals on how much to put aside for charity. Decide on who should be the beneficiary of your resources. While setting these goals, bear in mind the need to give out of love and expecting nothing in return.

Financial goals:

Money can change people at any moment. Money imbalance is bound to occur with couples, especially when both of you earn differently. It is very important to discuss each other's money habits and work on them. Both partners should be involved in making decisions about their finances.

Choose S.M.A.R.T goals:

Every marriage goals should include the S.M.A.R.T principles. All physical, intellectual, social, spiritual and financial goals should always be centered on these principles;

- **S** - Specific (We will go on a date night each week.)
- **M** - Measurable (Are we meeting our budget each month?)
- **A** - Achievable (Set aside 5% of our income for emergencies)
- **R** - Realistic (Communicate with each other on a daily basis)
- **T** - Time Conscious (In 5 years we will have our first child)

PRINCIPLE #2

Know the Mission

I was reading an article a few years ago that talked about the importance of businesses having a mission statement. The article went on to say that most businesses do not take any time to meaningfully define the overall mission/vision of the organization. They may have a mission statement but it just checks the box for having one.

Most businesses may not understand how critical it is to have a strong mission and vision for the business. In some cases, businesses may fail or perform poorly because they lack the vision and mission that would shape their strategic direction. When my husband and I agreed that we wanted to get married and spend the rest of our lives together, we never really thought about having a mission or vision for our marriage. We just believed that we would work toward the same goals and aspirations as a couple.

We really never sat down and talked about what we wanted for our marriage – what was driving those goals and aspirations. I think we felt that because we wanted it to work out, somehow it would. We thought that all we needed was unconditional love and everything else would take care of itself – we were so wrong about that.

Later in our marriage, we finally figured out that we needed to have a clear mission and vision for our marriage. That mission would guide everything that we did. That mission would set the overall course for our union together. When we needed to make major decisions about our kids, jobs, relocations, money, family, and any other issues, we would refer to our mission for the marriage.

I recall my husband had a job offer in Tampa, Florida. At the time, we were living in College Station, Texas. We had to make a difficult decision – he left a successful job that he loved, and we left a community that we knew well, to move to Florida to an unknown situation. In making the decision, we had to rely on our goals and mission for our marriage. We thought about one of our goals, which was living close to family. Tampa, Florida was only a 3.5-hour drive from where my husband's parents lived. They were both up in age, and we wanted our children to be able to visit their grandparents more often.

By relying on our mission and vision, it made that decision to leave Texas much easier. We have lived in Tampa for over 13 years and it was one of the best decisions that we have made. We were able to be by the sides of his parents when they both passed away. If we were still living in Texas, that would have never happened. By staying true to our mission, we were able to make a decision that we both agreed on and that worked out in a monumental way.

It does not matter what type of business you are running, understanding the vision and mission is critical. This sets the stage for every situation and every decision that you make. It also provides employees with an overall purpose that aligns with the organization. The mission and vision of an organization are so critical because both are used to define all of the goals and tactics that will be used for success.

Understanding the mission of the marriage helps to determine its overall direction. It allows the couple to focus their combined efforts toward a unified future. The mission also helps with decision making. There will be some very difficult decisions that will need to be made. A clearly outlined mission makes those decisions easier to handle. *Does this decision help us get to the overall mission of our marriage*? If the answer is no, then you should not move in that direction.

The mission also serves as a way to bring about alignment and agreement for the couple. As with businesses and their mission statements, it helps to shape the overall strategy of the marriage. The mission is the blueprint for the strategy. The other piece of this centers around evaluation. If you do not have a mission, plan, or vision, it will be more difficult to assess if you are headed in the right direction. Having a clear mission/vision helps determine what things to evaluate. *Are we doing the things that are necessary for our marriage to be successful?*

Many companies also have mission statements that bring everyone together for a common goal and purpose. My husband works at the Moffitt Cancer Center in Tampa, Florida. I think they have an excellent mission statement because it is short, direct and clear. Their mission is: "To contribute to the prevention and cure of cancer." Because it is clear and concise, every employee knows what the mission is. I believe it is important for marriages to have clear mission statements as well. A marriage mission statement might read something like:

- To commit to each other and work together as a team.

- To live a life with each other that makes us both better.

- To create a life together that will be built on love and trust.

- To set good examples for our children and raise them to be productive citizens.

- To respect and love our family and friends to the best of our ability.

- To live together in a Christ-like manner and allow God to provide the overall guidance and direction for everything that we do.

- To love, honor and cherish each other for the rest of our lives.

Marriage is a union and partnership between two people. Once couples say "I do", they should become one. But like any relationship, the individuals in the marriage are different and come to the table with contrasting strengths and weaknesses. These differences should be considered when working to understand each person's core values – another critical part of identifying and defining the mission statement of the marriage.

Core values are the things that matter most to each person and, consequently, to the couple. The couple should take some time to sit and discuss what their individual and collective core values are. Having an agreed-upon list will be instrumental in developing the mission and vision of the marriage. This is discussed in more detail in the chapter on culture.

The mission and vision help to direct the overall strategy of the marriage. It also helps to define the overall purpose of the marriage. The mission and vision also defines what the couple feels are the important aspects of the marriage. By understanding the mission and vision, you can put the steps and strategies in place that help to achieve that mission and vision. This clarity in the mission and vision ensures that the married couple can focus their energy and efforts towards that mission instead of unproductive distractions.

What are some examples of the mission or goals? Is it to live a happy life together? To have a great sex life? To be financially secure? To have a certain number of kids and to raise them appropriately? To never get a divorce? To be able to travel around the world together? To live life together as best friends? There are so many aspects of the mission of the marriage.

It will be up to the couple to establish what that mission is and just how detailed or multifaceted it will be. It could be all of the above missions or just one. The key is to be focused and committed to that mission once it is agreed upon.

One way of looking at the mission is to determine how it affects each individual in the marriage. One couple might say that their mission is to make each other better – to live together in a way that makes each other better in every aspect of life.

Your mission could be about faithfulness. You want to live a life where you are faithful to each other. You want a marriage in which there will be no worries about infidelity. Once you agree that your goal is to be faithful, there should be nothing that will pull you out of being loyal to each other. It's important to note that commitment plays a role here as well. Sticking to your mission statement means that you and your spouse will be 100% committed to each other.

In developing the mission and vision for your marriage, you must understand completely that marriage is a marathon and not a sprint. You and your spouse will work at your marriage in a way that implements that principle. It will take work and dedication to make the marriage as successful as it can be. Know and understand that viewing marriage as a marathon will help you stay focused on your long-range efforts and plans. Couples need to understand that they will be in this for the long haul, and they must be patient with each other. Everything will not always work out the way that they may want but if they exercise patience, they can get through tough times.

Understanding the mission also helps each spouse clarify the expectations of the marriage. The worst thing that could happen is that two individuals have a different set of expectations. The mission helps clarify what the expectations are for the marriage and for each individual in the marriage.

So, the first thing that couples need to do is specify the mission and vision of the marriage, as this sets the stage for all other aspects of the union.

Clarifying Your Expectations

It is not unusual for potential couples to have loads of expectations of their spouse. They still have this idea of a blissful courtship and a continual honeymoon which are expectations that they carry throughout the course of the marriage. This is quite understandable because most unrealistic expectations arise from the number of romantic books read or the movies seen. Remember your marriage is not a movie – it is real life.

There are common expectations most partners carry into their relationship;

- That your partner must always understand your point of view.
- Your partner should always be completely selfless and loving.
- Your partner should always agree to your desires and choices.
- Your partner should always be available whenever you need them.

- Your partner is responsible for your happiness.
- There should never be arguments or conflicts in a marriage.
- Your marriage should heal your childhood trauma.

These are few among the numerous unrealistic expectations of marriage. Having unrealistic expectations could bring up resentment during the course of the relationship and leave you disappointed in your partner. You must know this – that your partner is human and can and will make mistakes.

The acknowledgment of this fact would eliminate every unrealistic expectation and make you work on improving your relationship with your partner instead of resorting to resentment. With marriage you can expect some disagreements and differences to occur over time. Conflicts should be expected and each partner must put effort into trying to work through them.

Having unrealistic expectations does not mean having poor expectations and accepting poor and demeaning treatment from your spouse, it does not mean settling for less. In fact, you are expected to have expectations to be treated with kindness, love, and respect from your partner. There should be no tolerance for physical or emotional abuse. Unrealistic expectations are about having a notion of who your partner should be without acknowledging their flaws; expecting your relationship to be a pathway to perfection and a fairy tale life-style.

You can build up *realistic* expectations by;

- Talking to your partner about any issues that you may have. State your concerns and your fears without the need to be confrontational.

- Creating quality time. Find time to be together and have conversations about things that are fun and interesting to the both of you.

- Dealing with your differences and try to understand them from each others point of view.

- Do not be selfish with your thoughts.

- Clarifying unmet needs. Do not stack up your needs and expect your partner to know about them because you share the same space.

- Acknowledging the needs of your partner.

- Seeking the help of a relationship coach or counselor if needed. It is very commendable to come up with expectations for your marriage – but those expectations must be realistic.

Monogamy and Marriage

The basic and most common expectation of marriage is the idea of fidelity – the fact that partners should be committed to each other until death do them part. The expectations of infidelity often arise from a sense of entitlement and overconfidence in our strengths.

Another ridiculousness of monogamy is the assumption that infidelity does not exist in a happy relationship. The reason for most cheating partners does not necessarily arise from the fact of sadness or lack of commitment, but from a deep desire to satisfy a selfish urge or the grasp of a new discovery. The paradox of marriage and monogamy supports the fact that marriage does not fulfill every desire and expectation of both partners which acknowledges the need to clarify expectations before saying "I DO." With that being the case, each partner must make the decision to remain completely committed to their partner even if they may not fulfil every desire or expectation. Here is where love becomes a choice and not an emotion.

However, when monogamy is not maintained, unforgiveness becomes the primary force which has destroyed many promising marriages. Once a spouse cheats, this often results in the end of the marriage. There are typically no given opportunities to check out what the problem actually is and how to work towards solving it. The only thing that could be devised from the premise of infidelity is the disappointment our partner has caused us and the fact that our expectations have been destroyed, which is often followed by withdrawal and resentment.

Also, the pressure to leave or stay that comes from family and friends can be overwhelming because the focus is on the choice of the other partner and not the cheating partner. Now, the decision to forgive or leave a cheating partner is left for the deceived partner. While making your decision you must try to ask relevant questions in hopes that your decision does not leave you resentful. You can endure the tough test of infidelity and rebuild your trust by doing the following:

- ***Practice gratitude:*** Infidelity will make you forget every good quality of your partner. They are no longer who you thought they were before the marriage; but whenever you feel consumed by betrayal, you can always take a moment to refocus on their strengths and make an effort to remember and appreciate their good qualities.

- ***Face your feelings:*** It is a fact that infidelity can hurt your feelings and you are within your rights to blame and judge your partner for hurting you. If you can pause for a moment and face your fears calmly, you will be surprised at how easy it is. Blaming your partner every moment for every slightest mistake is just a method often used to overcome your fears and this method might cost you your sanity and your relationship

- ***Clarify your expectations:*** Expecting your partner to be perfect is unrealistic. You have to acknowledge the fact that your partner is human and human beings are bound to err. Instead of accumulating a list of every unmet expectation and sinking into a sea of disappointments, you could find solutions to making your marriage work again.

- ***Be vulnerable:*** It is common for the deceived partner to become emotionally bankrupt after infidelity is exposed. Those feelings you initially had for your partner appear to be gone. Take the risk to develop a fresh level of intimacy for your partner, stop trying to stifle your feelings and just allow yourself to breathe.

- ***Spend time together:*** Rediscover enjoyable things you can do together. Doing and enjoying those little activities that were once neglected might be a step in rebuilding your relationship.

- ***Reconnect the past to the future:*** You once had plans for your marriage. This is the time to go back to them and find ways of making them work. Thinking about your future again can rekindle the deep love you once had and develop a new era of intimacy and bonding.

- *Acknowledge your feelings:* Infidelity can bring up self-doubt. Maybe you are not good enough? Maybe you are not as beautiful as you had thought? All these feelings will come but you must know that you are never the cause of your partner's infidelity. People cheat based on their own volition, no matter what comes up, do not ever blame yourself.

- *Ask relevant questions:* Asking questions about who they cheated with or pushing your partner to compare you to them will not help you. Although this urge always comes up, do try to suppress it. Focus on your relationship.

- *Do not make hasty decisions:* Your first instinct may be to leave or go to confront your spouse's affair partner. Try to think before making decisions and weigh the pros and cons. Your first instinct might not be the wisest.

- *Be on the lookout:* As partners, both of you should work to prevent further episodes of infidelity. Identify each step that lead to its occurrence and map out safety measures against them.

- *Admit:* This is actually the first step for healing. The offending partner must be honest about why you made the decision to cheat. Be completely transparent and willing to answer all of your partners questions.

- *It is okay to cry:* Pour out your feelings as much as you can, you will be fine.

- *Rebuild trust:* Be resolute in your decisions of making your relationship work again. Also, the cheating partner should immediately stop all contact with the affair partner.

- ***Seek professional help:*** You can seek the assistance of a marriage coach or counselor whenever it seems too difficult to handle.

- ***Start afresh:*** Begin your relationship from the moment you both first met. Let go of the past pains and decide to begin a new relationship with your partner.

PRINCIPLE #3

Know Your Customer/ Know Your Spouse

You would not go into business with a person without first researching them and meeting with them to discuss business plans and goals. Your values, goals, and personalities should match up in a way that would increase the likelihood of success. Just like you research or vet your business partner before merging or going into business with them, you need to do the same type of legwork for your marriage.

While starting up a business, one does not randomly pick who will become their partner. You have to really know who you are doing business with – learn their strengths and weaknesses, where they can work efficiently and excel at their job. You must have this information before any agreement of partnership is done. How well do you know your partner? What are their strengths and their weaknesses? What are their habits that you could either live with or live without?

By knowing your partner, this will help you to determine if they are the right person for you. However, while trying to get to know your partner you must keep an open mind and remember that no relationship or marriage is perfect.

Be sure you know who you are marrying. It's true that you will learn more about your spouse as time passes but doing a little homework prior to the marriage could help you determine how compatible the two of you are. Spend a lot of time discussing each other's dreams, goals, morals, and values.

Spend quality time together, arrange to have dinner with some of his or her oldest and closest friends, take a trip to their hometown, request to meet family members, try out some of each other's hobbies and create new hobbies together. This will not reveal everything about your spouse, but it will give you some in-depth knowledge about their background – their family, friends, likes and dislikes.

Men and women are definitely different. It does not take a rocket scientist to figure this out. Women communicate and socialize differently and their wants and needs are different from men. Women need to feel loved. When women feel loved, they are able to return that love openly and honestly and nurture those around them. And listen men: when the woman is feeling nurtured and loved, that is when the sex is abundant!

She wants to know that she can count on you. She wants to feel like she can confide in you and trust you with her deepest secrets and innermost thoughts. This will not only facilitate the growth of the relationship but can also help to heal old wounds.

Women desire intimacy and need it from their spouse. They desire hand-holding, touching, hugging and kissing without always expecting sex as an end result. However, women also desire and need sexual intimacy. Remind her frequently of how beautiful she is and let her know that you continue to be physically and sexually attracted to her. I promise you, you both will benefit.

Men need and desire praise and approval from their spouse. Men need to feel loved and respected. Men need emotional intimacy but have a greater need and desire for sexual intimacy. When a man is having frequent and fulfilling sex, he has a general feeling that everything in the relationship is okay. And as loving and attentive as men can be, they also need their space. Wives, please do not take this as a sign of them falling out of love. Time alone allows him room for reflection, personal development, and growth, which are all things that are necessary for a healthy marriage.

Aside from understanding and navigating the unique needs of the sexes, there are some key ways you can learn more about your partner while also respecting their differences, becoming a better spouse, and strengthening your marriage.

- ***Ability to read your customer/spouse:*** As a married couple, you have to learn to prioritize your spouse's feelings and sideline your own. This means understanding how your spouse expresses their mental and emotional states when they're happy and when they're not. It's important for you to be able to identify when they are angry, tired, scared, hurt or afraid.

   Overlooking these signals could lead you into unnecessary conflicts or cause pain that could have been avoided. For example, if you had a great day at work and you're excited to tell your wife about a big deal you closed, but you notice that she's a bit sad when you walk in, don't proceed with your good news. Take a temperature check and investigate – figure out what's wrong. Show her that you're invested and that you're aware that something's not right. Together, you can talk about it and work toward a solution. And at some point, the coast will be clear for you to share your good news.

- ***Be empathetic:*** This is intertwined with the previous point. Being able to read your partner requires empathy. This means you're not only willing to listen but you can also show care and concern. You can stand in your partner's shoes and understand that they need help. Your spouse's problems are your problems, too, even if you didn't cause them or they don't directly affect you. A little bit of empathy will help bring resolution to almost any problem. Even if the problem is not solved, it will make your spouse feel better just knowing that you listened and that you were genuinely concerned. Here, you both learn a lot about one another.

- *Words of affirmation:* Your marriage is many things, and among them, it's a support system. As individuals, we use words of affirmation to boost our self-esteem. Think of times when you've told yourself, "I will have a positive day" or "I am worthy of success." Words of affirmation from a partner matter just as much. These words give you both the assurance that your marriage is sound, that it's your refuge, and that you will have protection when you need it most. Maybe this looks different for every couple (e.g. a card to express love or a text message), but what matters most is that these words exist and that they're shared with intent.

- *Gifts:* You don't want to place too much value on material things, but gifts both big and small show your spouse that you care. Buying a gift requires thought, time, money, and strategizing. For the person receiving the gift, it's not just about the gift itself but also the effort that went into selecting it. For example, if your wife has complained about sore or achy muscles and you give her a gift certificate to a spa for a massage, she'll appreciate it. Of course, the massage will help her feel better, but she also knows that you listened to her and found a gift that doubled as a solution.

- *Acts of service:* In the community, we engage in acts of service to show that we care – volunteering at a soup kitchen, running errands for the elderly, mentoring a young child. You can also perform acts of service in your marriage. Maybe this means cooking dinner on a night that you normally wouldn't, or picking up the dry cleaning, or preparing your spouse's coffee exactly how they like it. Acts of service are small acts of kindness that reinforce your commitment.

- *Quality time:* Your approach to quality time can teach you both a lot about one another. Quality time is time where you're focused on one another, either engaging in a new activity, catching up with each other, or just getting away from the daily grind. You remove distractions and center each other in your lives for a set amount of time. Your ability to do this on a regular basis means you'll get to know each other on a deeper level. You'll also form new experiences and memories together that strengthen your bond and teach you more about how you each react or behave in different scenarios.

- *Physical touch:* Knowing your spouse means engaging in physical touch. Right away, you might think about sexual intimacy. But physical touch can be smaller – a kiss on the cheek, a hand on the small of your back, a squeeze of the shoulder, a hug. Physical touch is a quick and easy yet meaningful way to show that you care. And how you and your spouse do this, and how you both react to it, can give you a new, nonverbal way to communicate effectively. If your husband normally kisses you goodbye before he heads to work, but he doesn't do it on this particular morning, it's an opening for you to make sure everything is ok with him. Physical touch is one of the strongest ways for you to connect with and learn about your spouse.

Intimate Knowledge About Your Spouse:

In any business, you must know your customers to grow your revenue. And you must know your business partners to create a productive work environment that fuels growth. In your marriage, you need that same level of recognition and understanding in order to truly know your spouse and ensure your union lasts.

You can get intimate knowledge of your partner by trying out these points:

Unravel their life story:

Do not jump to the conclusion yet. Because he speaks softly does not guarantee the start-up of a beautiful love story. Dig deeper and unravel things about them that would be good to know as you learn each other. This would help you know if the two of you are compatible. Meanwhile, you also have to prepare your mind to accept or not accept any discoveries you may find.

Check out their dislikes:

Each person has a set of habits that may be annoying. In as much as these could be seen as no big deal, they may be so irritating that it causes friction in the relationship. Lovingly discuss each annoying habit and try to come up with a resolution. Try to remember that your partner is a different person with a totally different set of life experiences from yours; and as a result of this, you must make some compromises and necessary adjustments.

Know what their triggers are :

Anger is relative. People react to situations differently mostly based on their temperament and life experiences. You can identify what makes your partner angry by the way they respond to certain situations. This is a good way of avoiding unnecessary arguments and improving your relationship.

The people and things that matter to them:

Make a list of their favorite things/activities and their favorite people. Spend time thinking of people, places and things that could easily make them smile. This is a thoughtful way of showing that you really care and this can also serve as a means of clarifying unrealistic expectations that their happiness comes from just you and your marriage.

What are their dreams and aspirations:

This part is a very important aspect of knowing who your partner really is. Marriage does not stop or limit dreams, it should rejuvenate ambitions and this is exactly when the other partner steps in. What are the goals and ambitions they had before the marriage? Encouraging your partner to pursue their dreams will also inspire you to do the same. It is such a great feeling seeing your partner soaring higher and reaching all their goals.

What makes them laugh deeply and sincerely:

This can be seen as petty but we will never realize what laughter can do as a part of the wellbeing of your partner. Recent studies have discovered that one of the most common qualities that most potential partners look out for is around having a sense of humor. Laughter massages the soul and gives positive energy to your spouse - so find ways to make your partner laugh deeply and often.

Understand their past relationships:

This particular subject of their past breakups will surface from time to time in your current relationship. Do not be put off easily by the tales of previous relationships. Although a lot of time should not be spent focusing on past relationships; you can gain a lot of information and knowledge about your partner through their past behaviors and interactions. Why did they break up, how did they handle stress or disagreements, were they needy or lazy? Have an open mind to accept the truth and the fact that you can not change them. But also take this time to evaluate what you've learned and decide if this is a person you want to spend the rest of your life with. If your partner was physically or verbally abusive in their past relationship, more than likely they are going to exhibit the same behaviors in this relationship. Perhaps your partner suffered a broken heart in their past relationship. Try to understand their pain and the fact that their love and trust had once been broken.

What are their core values:

Every individual possesses a set of values that defines them. It could be honesty, accountability, transparency, loyalty, integrity, etc. They hold these values in high esteem and are likely never to compromise them. Respect their values and be willing to vouch for them anywhere - you can only do this when you are fully aware of who they really are as well as their capabilities.

Spark up their crazy side:

Even the most melancholic individual has their own crazy side. This sweet crazy side adds more excitement to the relationship and should not be left unnoticed. Learn their pattern of "crazy" and when they usually switch to that side. Enjoy every moment while discovering amazing traits within your partner.

What is their take on marriage and the future:

Unfortunately many couples tend to wander aimlessly in their relationship. They are not sure if they are part of their potential partner's future decisions. Ask the right questions and talk about your life together and what you want it to look like in five, ten or twenty years. Their responses and reactions will tell you if they are focusing on goals of longevity.

The list of things you should know about your partner is not an exhaustive list and it is mostly dependent on your partner and the relationship you share. No two relationships are the same. However, if you are able to satisfactorily learn as much about your partner as possible, then you are working efficiently towards improving your marriage and increasing your chances of enjoying a long and healthy relationship.

PRINCIPLE #4

Great Communication Is Key

Great communication is one of the foundations of a successful business. Great communication is the foundation of a strong marriage. Great communication skills are key to success in life, work, and relationships. At work, being able to communicate effectively with superiors, co-workers, and staff is essential regardless of what line of work you are in. In marriage, being able to communicate effectively with your spouse is necessary in order to facilitate growth and longevity in the relationship.

When there is trouble at work, such as misunderstandings or differences of opinion, being able to talk about the issues (perhaps with the aid of a mediator) will help resolve them. If you don't address the problem, then the elephant in the room will only grow bigger and bigger and the same is true in marriage. Couples need to be able to talk about what's bothering them and do so while remaining calm and respectful to each other.

If the issues are tough and cannot be resolved, a mediator may be necessary to bring about conflict resolution. Ignoring the issues or sweeping them under the rug won't make the elephant in the room go away. Being able to tackle the issues will keep the communication lines clear and help keep the marriage strong.

The same communication mistakes that can cause havoc on the job are the same communication mistakes that can cause instability in marriage. Some of these mistakes are:

- Not listening

- Speaking before you've had time to think

- Raising your voice

- Using degrading language

- Refusing to take responsibility for your actions
- Using negative nonverbal communication

Not listening/waiting to take your turn:

One of the most important communication skills is the ability to listen. No one likes communicating with a person who is always talking and won't let the other person get a word in. At work, if you're not a good listener, you will more than likely miss important instructions and make mistakes that could have otherwise been avoided. In a marriage, if you refuse to listen, you will miss critical information and some nonverbal cues which indicate how your spouse is truly feeling.

Think before you speak:

When communicating at work or within your marriage, you should always take time to let the information you receive marinate before responding. I call this 'take 2.' Take two deep breaths; inhale and exhale twice, and give yourself time to prepare an appropriate response instead of producing an inappropriate reaction.

Schedule times for you and your spouse to discuss important family matters and individual issues that are important to each of you. When the communication stops flowing, the union is negatively impacted and the marriage begins a downward spiral.

Turn down the volume:

Typically, when we raise our voices, it's a pretty accurate indicator that we are angry; unless we are at a sporting event, concert or some other venue that is loud and noisy and causes us to talk louder than usual. During a conversation, the tone, volume and pitch of your voice all indicate the type of energy and emotion that you are using while communicating.

We would probably think twice before raising our voice at our boss or co-workers. And if we did encounter a split second of lack of self-control, we would be quick to offer an apology and explanation as to why this happened. Your spouse deserves the same amount of respect. When we are having conversations with our spouses, sometimes things escalate, emotions run high and we raise our voices to try to get our point across or to drown out what our spouse is trying to say. Raising your voice may be interpreted as verbally aggressive, which may be counteracted with a similar response or it might alienate your spouse and cause feelings of anger and resentment.

Choose your words wisely:

I think most of us have been close to losing or have actually lost our cool on the job and in our marriage. Using degrading language while talking to your boss, your co-workers or your spouse will bring about the end of a good thing pretty quickly. You should never engage in verbal abuse.

When I have been in mediation with couples, trying to help bring about a resolution to a problem, a common quick reaction was the threat of divorce or the discussion of separation. Though the partner in question likely didn't mean it, these kinds of threats or insults can leave a lasting impression.

Refusing to take responsibility for your actions:

It is a fact that all of us have made mistakes. We have all made poor choices. It is critical that we take responsibility for these actions. If we neglect to take responsibility for our mistakes and poor choices, it will be difficult for us to develop self-respect and gain the respect of others. And typically, a person who does not accept responsibility for their words and actions finds it very easy to blame others. When you exhibit a pattern of not taking responsibility and repeatedly blaming others, you are seen as a liability on your job and you become a liability in your marriage.

Accepting responsibility is indicative of a person's true character. When you voluntarily come forth, tell the truth and apologize (if necessary), this is an indication of the type of person you really are. Taking responsibility for your words and actions will help you gain huge merits at work and will provide a forum for open and honest communication in your marriage. Don't fixate on mistakes. When you make a mistake (and as previously mentioned, we all do), admit that you made a mistake, offer an apology, take the necessary actions to rectify it (if applicable) and move on.

One way to get out of taking responsibility for your actions is to bring up your partner's past mistakes or offenses. This is an avoidance behavior that temporarily takes the spotlight off of you and casts a light of blame and shame over your spouse. There is a great quote that I like that applies here: *"When you blame others, you give up your power to change." (Author Unknown)*

Negative nonverbal communication

Actions speak louder than words. Do you know that the majority of our communication is nonverbal? We do a lot of communicating with facial expressions, body gestures and eye contact. These nonverbal communications fall under a subcategory of physical communication, which is the most used form of nonverbal communication.

These include things such as the distance you put between you and the person you are communicating with, folding your arms, crossing your legs, the strength of your handshake, hugging, patting someone on the back or any other type of physical touch. Of course, the way in which you present these behaviors will determine how they are perceived.

If you are having an intense conversation with your boss or co-worker, and in the middle of the conversation you roll your eyes or turn your back towards them, we can pretty much conclude that there will be some type of negative response or reaction from your boss or co-worker. The same holds true for similar behaviors that are exhibited during a conversation with your spouse.

Your body language sends off loads of information regardless of the words you are saying. If you are tense, frowning, avoiding eye contact and constantly looking at your watch, these all send very strong signals to your spouse that the last thing you want to do at that moment is to have a conversation.

Eye contact is also widely used in nonverbal communication. The eyes are considered a window into a person's thoughts, and many times, you can tell exactly what a person is feeling by how they are looking.

Agree to Disagree

Let me start this off by saying that you and your spouse will never agree on every single thing. But this doesn't have to be a bad thing. Just because you don't see eye to eye on every issue doesn't mean that you need to start looking for divorce lawyers. You both are individuals and you have your own individual thoughts, opinions, and experiences.

When you can't find consensus, you have to agree to disagree. Oftentimes in business, there will be conflict, differences of opinion and differences in thoughts on strategic direction. In order to move forward in spite of differences, the business leaders must agree to disagree. In cases like this, the overall goal of the business is more important than if the individual is right or wrong. The same holds true in the marriage.

In order to do this, each spouse must be able to voice their opinion and feel like they are being heard. There are a few things that each of you will have to do in order to make this work. First, review what the issue is to be sure you both have a clear understanding of what you are disagreeing about. Then decide who will voice their opinion first.

Next, be sure that you don't interrupt when your spouse is talking. Each of you should be actively listening while the other is talking, which not only demonstrates respect but may also allow you to hear something that you haven't heard before. This may help clear up any misunderstandings.

And guess what? When you agree to disagree, you both are winners!! That's right! Neither one of you is right or wrong. You both have an opinion and it just so happens to be different on this particular issue. So, what do you do? Try not to take it personally. Recognize that when your spouse is rejecting your opinion, he or she is not rejecting you. You must realize that having a difference of opinion is okay; agree to disagree and move on. What you shouldn't do is get angry and try to convince your spouse that you are right and they are wrong. This will build resentment and frustration and may lead to marital problems.

Remember that love covers a multitude of sins, mistakes, and disagreements. Be sure that you are showing your spouse love and respect. Remember that prayer is the great equalizer and a strong prayer life will bring about solutions to many problems.

You don't have to agree on everything in order to have a healthy, happy marriage. But if your disagreements are over your core morals, values and beliefs, then marriage coaching or counseling may be necessary.

Forgive and Forget

When there is offense, hostility, and resentment in the workplace, it needs to be dealt with immediately. There are many strategies that can be implemented in order to address the issue, such as defining the problem, listening to both sides, trying to find common areas of agreement and looking for solutions to the problem. But in order to restore healthy work relationships and continued productivity, forgiveness, letting go and moving on are definitely required. The same thing holds true for the marital relationship.

Being able to forgive and forget is a critical tool for a healthy marriage. Forgiveness is a process and it is a commitment to personal change and growth. Forgiving your spouse does not mean that the hurt or offense did not happen and it does not mean that they are right and you are wrong. Forgiveness is a way of detaching yourself from the hurt or offense and it allows you to move forward instead of holding on to the past.

Forgiveness is more beneficial for you than it is for the other person. Unforgiveness can lead to depression, stress, hostility, anxiety, sleep disorders and a whole list of other medical issues. It can also lead to the demise of the marriage. When you forgive your spouse, you facilitate an environment for a healthy relationship.

When you forgive and move past the issue, you are able to heal and move on with your life. Unresolved bitterness and resentment can take dominion over you. Remember, forgiveness is a choice and by choosing to forgive, you will feel less like the victim and regain your sense of power. Forgiveness is healthy for you and your relationship. Forgiveness is good for you mentally and physically, and it restores positive feelings, thoughts, and behaviors toward your spouse.

Using Economic Approaches to Managing Conflicts in Marriage

There are various economic principles that can be applied to businesses especially when it has to do with managing profits and losses. These principles provide a platform for the growth of the business and a stronger relationship with your business partners. Since marriage is a business that may involve arising conflicts, applying these economic principles could be of benefit to make it successful.

The various economic principles involve:

1. *The scale of preference:*
In business, the scale of preference involves the listing of needs according to a scale of priorities. Every business owner knows what is needed by the customers according to every season so they draw a scale of preference with needs that demand immediate attention on the top list. For married couples it could be kids, rent, mortgage, healthcare, education, food, etc. This could also include placing

your partner as your number one priority. Most partners tend to place unnecessary things on their list before their partners, which always results in disagreement and sometimes separation. Find out what is needed most in your relationship. What are the problems that need to be tackled immediately? Do not suppress any need or wait till it adds up and becomes difficult to tackle. Also, as you draw out your scale of preference, be sure to fully involve your spouse. This could be a very powerful exercise that will ensure that both of you are on the same page.

2. Cost-benefit analysis:

This principle is relevant in decision making. Cost-benefit analysis involves the action that follows a decision made by the business analysts - the merits and demerits. For instance, a business owner would have to evaluate and analyze the decision to embark on any project. The outcome of the evaluation will determine whether the project would be done or not. In marriage, applying cost-benefit analysis is very essential in making the decision about date nights, vacations, mortgages, rent, car payments, raising kids, etc.

Both partners must ensure the decision is financially feasible and would not outweigh their capabilities before proceeding to carry out the decisions. Cost-benefit analysis can be managed through savings which can be set aside each week or month before the date of the decided activity.

3. Choice theory:

This involves the clashing of choices of both business partners where either partner wants different things. In this case, one choice needs to be accepted not for the benefit of the supposed partner but for the benefit of the company. This theory uses interactive strategies that might either outplay one of the choices of the partner or both choices. In order to avoid conflict between partners, a point of neutral equilibrium should be reached where both partners play a part in producing results. The choice theory can be very disturbing because both partners would always want different things and neither of them would want to surrender.

However, there are three strategies that you could use as a guide when in conflict with your partner as a result of choice theory:

- Strive for the best results. It is tempting to want your choice to be accepted regardless of its effect on your partner, but you must acknowledge the fact that your choice might possibly not be the best choice for the relationship. So strive for the results that benefit your marriage.

- Consider your partner and how it would affect them and let this guide your behavior towards making choices.

- Put yourself in the same condition. What if it were your choice that has to be discarded? What if your partner strongly insists on their choice instead of yours regardless of your feelings?

4. *Incentives:*

Incentives are always used in business to motivate consumers. It encourages them to patronize the business more often. Incentives can also be given to the employees which helps in motivating their behavior and attitude towards work. In marriage, incentives should come up in various ways; thanking your partner for helping out with the chores would encourage them to do more, acknowledging their efforts and gestures in becoming a better person would motivate them to strive more. Being kind to your partner and extending unexpected gestures would boost the positivity of the relationship.

5. *Microeconomics:*

Microeconomics deals with the smallest details of a business that are often neglected. It studies the costs and benefits of small changes. Going out of your comfort to rebrand your products to the consumer's taste might be a small change but can as well boost the growth of your business. It will be critically important for the couple to pay attention to the small details of the marriage. Sometimes it can be the small details that go unchecked that can cause significant issues within the marriage. For example, one couple shared with me that there was an issue with the husband not opening doors for the wife. He would not open building doors or car doors for her. If he opened a building door he would go in first. He never opened the car door. It was a small thing that the wife did not like but she never expressed how it made her feel. When she finally confronted him many years later he was so mad that it caused him to become resentful. It was a small matter that went unchecked for many years that brought about some serious issues in the marriage.

Benefits of an Active Listener

Being a good listener involves active and attentive listening. The difference between a passive listener and an active listener is that a passive listener listens to respond and react while an active listener listens to become involved in the conversation.

You can become an active listener by:

- Being truly engaged in the discussion.

- Avoid the distraction of thinking about yourself during the conversation.

- Using non-verbal communication such as eye contact, nodding, and smiling to show you are engaged in the conversation.

- Avoid dishing out advice in the middle of the conversation. Most times people come to you, not for advice, but need a passionate listener. Rather than give advice, you can ask them questions that would involve them in solving their own problems.

- Validate their experiences and emotions when appropriate.

Here are the benefits of active listening in a relationship:

- Improves communication between partners.

- Creates a safe space for a true conversation without judgment.

- Harmonizes the relationship with your partner.

- Increases intimacy between partners.

- Helps you develop patience and tolerance.

- Good and active listening increases the odds of having a long-lasting and productive relationship.

Business Language and Love Language

The success of every business is dependent on the language of communication; the way by which you interact with your customers. Language is a powerful tool when it comes to building excellent customer service skills. The use of your language in business determines the feedback of your customers whether negative or positive. Customers need to feel engaged while having conversations with their service provider; they need to feel that they matter.

Languages used in communication can also be seen in sending emails and memos which determines whether the customer would respond negatively or positively to the message. Positive language is the key to a positive customer service experience. The use of love languages is encouraged in every relationship during communication and should be centered on what I call the *3Cs*:

- C - Complement - You must be ready to assist and complete every action expected from your partner.

- C- Compromise - Create a comfortable climate for change even if it infringes a little upon your space.

- C- Compliment - Encourage by complimenting and saying positive things to your spouse. Avoid nagging and condemning every mistake.

- Now take a look at your relationship. How do you communicate with your partner? What tone of language do you use when correcting your partner?

Love language is the code of communication used in talking to your partner as well as actions that you take in order to make them feel loved. There are five love languages that we briefly touched on in an earlier chapter. These are love languages according to Dr. Garry Chapman in his book, *"The 5 love languages:"*

Words of Affirmation:

It makes use of verbal compliments that expresses love and build up your partner's self-esteem.

"I love your hair cut."

"You look incredible in those pants."

"I always enjoy your company."

Acts of Service:

This one focuses more on practice. You do not only get to compliment your partner but also help them in becoming a better person. This love language is intentional about your partner's happiness and ultimate satisfaction, it is not done out of obligation. Acts of services can include; doing laundry, babysitting, cooking dinner, grocery shopping, picking up the kids from school, etc.

Receiving Gifts:

You can just pick up your partner's favorite ice-cream, send them some flowers or give a leg massage. The ultimate intent of this love language is not about material gifts but a simple gesture that will make your partner feel loved.

Quality Time:

This love language is focused on your partner. They have to be at the center of your attention. It does not necessarily mean going out on a date or participating in some other planned activity. You could just curl up on the bed or on the couch 'Netflixing' with popcorn and ice cream. No phone calls, chatting, texting, it is just you and your partner.

Physical Touch:

Most couples want to feel close to each other because it makes them feel connected and safe in the relationship. Frequent hugging, kissing, fondling, holding hands is encouraged for partners whose primary love language is physical touch. It does not have to be sex.

Each individual/partner has their own preferred love language. Learning your partner's primary language and your own love language will not only boost your relationship goals, it will also create a stronger intimacy between you and your partner.

Characteristics of Love Languages

- Love languages are unconditional.

- Love languages involve realistic actions: Telling your partner to stop seeing their family because of a selfish reason is unrealistic. It is very likely not going to work.

- Love languages offer choices instead of limitations: "Would you like to go see a movie with me?"

- Love language is encouraging and not condescending.

- Love language is simple to grab and not complicated.

Here are a few commendable tones of love languages that can be used in communication:

- "I have been thinking about our relationship lately and I feel we need to make adjustments on certain issues; would you give a suggestion on how we could tackle our issues?"

- "I know your friends are a very important aspect of your life and I would not want to come between you and them, but I would love it if you create more time for both of us."

- "I am always here for you and I am willing to go through this with you."

Falling into the trap of nagging and always condemning your partner's action is easy but you can learn the use of love languages when communicating with your spouse. It makes your relationship beautiful and mature.

Talking Straight in Your Relationship

As clichéd as it may sound, communication remains the key to every relationship, not just communication but good and straightforward communication. Being a good communicator in your relationship involves using words that would make your partner listen to you.

A good communicator has the ability to convey their feelings in a healthy way; it has to come with connection and passion. If you're only waiting for your partner to finish talking so it could be your turn, then you are not a good communicator. The key to being a good communicator in your relationship is not actually the use of words but the use of both words and the ability to listen to your partner.

You can achieve great communication in your relationship through the following ways:

- ***Be open and honest:*** Express your feelings clearly; say what you mean and mean what you say. Avoid cutting corners, this may confuse your partner and make them not want to listen to you.

- ***Do not be scared of potential conflicts:*** Conflicts in marriages are bound to happen, so do not be scared of the disagreements that may occur in the process of expressing yourself. The conflicts will end as you and your spouse will either agree or agree to disagree. Do not bury your emotions.

- ***Speak calmly:*** When you find yourself talking fast, you should take a deep breath and begin talking again; this time slowly, in order to clearly get your message across.

- *Ask open-ended questions:* Ask questions that require more than a "yes" or "no" answer. Try to get details without pressuring them. Instead of asking "did you had a good day at work?," try asking "what happened at work today?" You could even be more specific; "How did the meeting go?"

- *Watch out for non-verbal expressions:* Take note of your partner's non-verbal cues. They may say "all is well" but they look upset, can't stop fidgeting or they may be avoiding eye contact. Listen to their tone of voice and their actions while speaking.

- *You do not have to read their minds:* In as much as you may think you know what is going in their mind, do not share what you think. Allow them to express themselves.

- *Conversations should not be a monologue:* Remember to take turns giving each other the opportunity to speak and be heard. If you do all the talking, you leave the conversation the same way you entered it, where nothing has changed. It will take both of you bring about conflict resolution.

Remember this! Communication is a skill that you can cultivate and there is always room for improvement. Work together with your partner and find ways to converse better.

Demonstrating Respect in Relationships

Showing equal respect is a great start-up for a healthy relationship. What might be seen as disrespect in your relationship might be fine in another relationship. Just remember if you respect yourself, it will be hard to accept other people disrespecting you.

What is self-respect? No one gives what they do not possess. Self-respect is the acceptance of yourself and everything that comes with finding ways to become a better person. It is the key to building a successful relationship with your partner.

Self-respect also means choosing to take care of your mind, body and spirit through eating healthy, engaging in physical activities and discovering new hobbies. Self-respect is a precursor to gaining mutual respect in your relationship.

The steps below will help in enhancing the level of respect with your partner:

- Be a good listener and stay attentive to your partner's desires and emotions.

- Show interest in your partner through your actions.

- Respond as quickly as possible to the requests of your partner if they are within your ability.

- Encourage your partner through your words and actions.

- Place a high value on confidentiality. Never share personal information or negative feelings about your spouse with family or friends unless given permission to do so.

- Work on your problems together and attempt to find solutions.

- Be patient and kind.

- Be a supportive partner.

- Be ready to forgive as well as ask for forgiveness.

- Show gratitude.

- Avoid unhealthy and unnecessary comparisons.
- Make the respect that you have for your partner known to everyone through your actions and words.

As I said earlier, great communication is critical to the success of any marriage or partnership. If you make communication a key pillar in your relationship, you are much more likely to have an overall successful marriage.

PRINCIPLE #5

Time Management

Do you and your spouse consider yourself a team? Most of us have probably been on some sort of team or in a group where success was dependent upon more than one person. Examples of this could be our current work teams, sports teams, debate teams, cheerleading teams, drill teams, choirs or singing groups, and the list goes on. The point here is that we have had to rely on other people in order to win or get the job done.

In the workplace, the team approach is definitely going to be most effective in the delivery of goods and services and maintaining the mission of the business. In order to obtain the most productivity, co-workers have to learn to work together. In order to work together effectively, each team member will have to understand their roles and responsibilities and this is also true for the marriage.

A successful marriage is all about teamwork. You and your spouse should be making team decisions on a daily basis, as to who will be responsible for completing certain tasks or who will take on certain responsibilities. In order for the marriage to be successful, both spouses have to share the load. Each spouse should have clear and established roles, but each role should allow for flexibility. Flexibility is essential in a healthy relationship because roles change naturally over time. The roles can also change when the needs of the family change. Examples: when a child is born; if a spouse or family member becomes ill; when the children leave for college; or if a spouse takes on additional work or a new job – these are all scenarios that could require one or both spouses to take on more than was initially agreed upon.

In order to make teamwork more natural and attainable in your marriage, I have listed three things below to assist you in your efforts:

1. Teamwork Makes the Dream Work:

Many of you have probably heard this catchy phrase, and I must say, it's one of my favorites. My son is a basketball player and during one of his games, I felt that some of his teammates were being "ball hogs" – they were not passing the ball to him and others who were positioned on the court to score. So, I stood up and yelled, "Teamwork makes the dream work!" Needless to say, my daughter (who was sitting next to me) was horrified and my son looked up in the bleachers from the court with a look on his face that basically said, "Mom, if you say that again, I'm going to ask the referees to put you out." End of story; they did not win because they did not use the team approach.

The Bible tells us in Ephesians 5:31: "For this reason, a man will leave his father and mother and be united to his wife, and the two will become one flesh." (NIV). This sounds like a team to me!

Each of you likely have your own individual goals and dreams that you want to achieve in life. But since you are partners and have shared values, morals, and goals, it would be easier to achieve success if you discussed your goals and dreams with each other as opposed to keeping them to yourself.

2. There Is No "I" In Team:

If you have been on a sports or work team, your coach or team leader has probably said this more times than you can remember, and it's absolutely true. When using the team approach, it's not about "I" but rather "we". In order to make the team work, you are going to have to be less concerned about yourself and more concerned about discussing and implementing what it will take to help each of you to achieve your goals.

3. Effort is Worth Something:

Make a concentrated effort to find out and address what each of you need in order to meet your individual goals. This does not contradict teamwork or your commitment to helping each other meet your goals. But as previously stated, each of you should also have your individual goals and you need to be clear about what you need from your spouse in order to achieve them.

Because you are employed, it's probable that more time is dedicated toward your job than to achieving and working on personal goals; although, in some instances, both can be addressed at the same time. But if this is not the case, and you find yourself with only enough time to eat, sleep and work, then measures have to be put in place so each of you has time to address personal needs and goals. For example, if the house is constantly a mess and it bothers one of you, it affects both of you. If neither one of you have the desire or the time to clean the house, you should hire someone to clean it for you. And although this is an added expense and can prove to be costly, it definitely is cheaper than marriage counseling and will provide an immediate solution to an apparent problem. Freeing up responsibilities should allow you time to work on your personal goals.

I have a set of friends who have been married for 20 years. The husband is self-employed and not looking to retire anytime soon but the wife is winding up a career in education and is looking to embark on a second career as a private chef and cooking instructor. They have two children; one is in middle school and the other is in high school. Both children are athletes and play on their school teams. The husband has established a routine of working late because his wife's work schedule has allowed her to get off work and pick up the kids from practices and games. But now the wife needs to take classes two nights a week in order to get the training and skills that she needs for her second career. It took more than a few conversations to come up with a schedule that allowed the wife to get the training that she desired and needed. Typically, when routines have been set, they are hard to break.

But true to what teamwork is all about, the husband agreed to adjust his schedule so he could leave his business early and pick up the kids one night a week. Arrangements were made with a friend to pick the kids up from school the other night. So, you see, just like you have to compromise and accommodate schedules and assignments at work in order to keep things fair and equitable and allow room for individual growth; the same should be expected and implemented in the marriage.

Time Management

One of the easiest things you can do for your marriage is managing the amount of time that you spend on yourself, with your spouse, with family, and with friends. Everything that you value – your marriage, children, work, family and friends – will become a chore if you do not manage them properly.

Time Alone

If you do not take care of yourself, you will not be able to adequately participate in the caring of others. If you are overcommitted, exhausted and grumpy, you will not enjoy your spouse or your family. Do not look at time alone as selfish. It will be necessary for you to get away in order to revive yourself and rejuvenate. Taking a little time away from the responsibilities of being a spouse or parent gives you a better perspective, renewed energy and a new appreciation for those you love.

Studies have shown that having alone time keeps the relationship healthy. In as much as intimacy is encouraged in the relationship between partners, there is another angle of intimacy that is also encouraged - self-intimacy. This is the time set aside for reflection, it enables you to reflect on who you are, what you really want, your strengths, your weaknesses, your fears, and your goals. This is a moment to free your mind from every distraction, it is time to let your guard down and give yourself the freedom to go deeper into yourself. Alone time is an opportunity to ask yourself relevant questions; questions that will help you in your relationship with your partner.

There are a few signs that show that you really need time for yourself:

- ***Picking on your partner over unnecessary things:*** Bickering over insignificant things shows you are stressed and need some space. Getting pissed over little things becomes routine because you are fed up with work and other issues, so you need room to breathe.

- ***Boredom:*** You want to go places and your spouse wants to stay at home. You want to watch a movie and your spouse wants to sleep. Too much of this, and you start to get bored, become frustrated and lose interest in trying to spend time with your spouse. If you are beginning to get bored with your spouse, you should voice your frustrations, discuss and look for activities that are interesting and enjoyable to the both of you. But you should also take this opportunity to venture out on your own and discover things that you would enjoy doing solo. This does not imply something is wrong with your partner or relationship. Alone time gives you the opportunity to refresh yourself and come back anew.

- ***Evaluate your friendships::*** Every couple should surround themselves with good friends to have fun and celebrate life's accomplishments and to offer consolation and support when needed. But if you have changed and some of your friends have not, and getting together with them is causing you more stress than joy; then it is probably time to re-evaluate those relationships. Maybe all you need is to adjust the frequency or amount of time you spend with these friends, or maybe you need to sever all ties. Making these kind of decisions can be difficult, but continuing unhealthy friendships/relationships can be detrimental to you and your marriage.

- ***You no longer feel like yourself:*** You have lost sight of who you really are as everything seems bleak. Consider giving yourself time to reconnect and come back to who you really are.

- ***Avoiding your hobbies:*** When was the last time you went to the gym? When was the last time you worked in your garden? Do not neglect the things that you enjoy; Creating time to enjoy yourself can help you enjoy life without having to rely on another individual.

We now know that alone time is needed and necessary. But sometimes we become so engrossed in our relationship that its hard for us to come up with things to do while we are alone. You could:

- ***Go for walks:*** Taking walks rejuvenates your spirit and brings awareness to nature.

- ***See your favorite band by yourself:*** This is a great way of reconnecting with old times and meeting new people.

- ***Learn something new:*** Focus on satisfying your interests. You could sign up for a class where you learn a new skill or hobby.

- ***Read books:*** This is the time to discover the magic in words. Get yourself engrossed in the beauty of good books.

- ***Volunteer:*** Take the time to respond to a need in your community. This will benefit your community and can benefit your psychological well-being.

Benefits of Spending Time Alone

1. It increases empathy:

Creating time for yourself will give you the capacity to care for others. You love others by first loving yourself; it is to love your neighbor as you love yourself.

2. It increases productivity:

Returning from vacation or time off has proven to increase productivity. Also, spending time alone improves your concentration and memory which helps you focus your attention on what needs to be done.

3. It improves creativity:

You are often better at producing effective results when you work on your own. Doing things alone increases your focus and innovative ability without added peer pressure.

4. *Time to re-discover yourself:*

Spending time alone gives you an opportunity to examine your life and recall all your dreams and plans. You find time to focus on your interests and find ways to achieve your dreams.

Cons of Spending Time Alone

There are cons to spending time alone when it becomes extreme and inconsiderate. When we neglect our obligations and the needs of our partner in the bid to spend time alone, it brings up disadvantages such as:

1. *Vulnerability to negative thoughts:*

Extreme isolation can bring up negative thoughts and self-doubts for you and your spouse. Too much time alone may be infringing upon selfishness and could also cause your spouse to be concerned.

2. *Loneliness:*

We can easily drift into loneliness when we overdo this process of spending time alone. Once you notice you are no longer enjoying the moment, stop and spend time doing things with your partner or with those around you.

3. *Depression:*

Isolation suppresses the energy to be positive. You stop hanging out with people who love you and care for you because you have low energy and low interest. They start to worry about you and express their concerns. If this happens, seek help and make every effort to return to being more engaged. Coaching or counseling may be needed.

However, spending time alone cannot be equated to loneliness. It involves acknowledging your partner and finding time for yourself amidst regular relationship interactions. Loneliness, on the other hand, places your partner aside and keeps them in the dark. Also, your time alone is not the moment to be negative. It is a time to look back at your life and be grateful for every good thing that has happened in your life and in your relationship.

Again, the only drawback of spending time alone is going overboard. If you spend too much time alone, not only will you be missed but your spouse may begin to feel like you are not adequately engaged in the relationship, which could cause feelings of resentment.

Date Night

Your life together cannot be all work and no play. Whatever things you enjoyed doing that brought you together, you should continue to enjoy doing as you stay together. This could include going out to dinner, going to the movies, taking walks in the park, exercising together, going on vacation or having a staycation.

Do not let children and work schedules be an excuse for not spending time together. Hire babysitters or ask family members to look after the children for a few hours while you and your spouse find time to reconnect. Or get up early and spend time together while the children are sleeping.

Spending time together and spending quality time together are two different things. If either or both of you work, by the time you get home, you are probably exhausted. And if you have children, then there's more work to do and less opportunity for quality time. So, you will have to be intentional about spending quality time with each other.

Setting boundaries will enable you to take better care of yourself and will help keep the relationship healthy. It's no easy feat to manage time for yourself, your spouse, your family, friends, and your job. But just as setting boundaries within your work helps keep you focused and helps keep things in perspective, setting boundaries within your marriage will provide the same level of focus and perspective to help you enjoy a healthy relationship.

Keep Learning

Remember we are never too old to learn something new. Learning new things as a couple keeps the marriage interesting and creates opportunities for growth and deeper bonding. Learning new things together may also help reenergize a relationship that has become routine and boring. While the two of you are sharing new experiences, you are also spending quality time together which will help to keep things interesting.

PRINCIPLE #6

Providing Safety and Security

It is imperative for businesses to provide a safe and secure environment for their employees. Many companies talk about a culture of safety. That means that everyone who is a part of the organization has a responsibility to have safety and security as a main priority. This is the case for those who you work with, the clients that you serve, or anyone who comes into your business. Everyone is responsible for safety and security. It involves looking after everyone that you come into contact with. When there is a situation that may be unsafe, employees are strongly encouraged to report the situation to a supervisor or someone who has the authority to address the problem.

Another aspect of safety and security in the workplace is **protecting the assets** of the organization. That refers to tangible items like data, money, and property, – anything that has value and would need to be protected or kept safe and secure. There is a major threat happening in the business world with people stealing data from companies. There is an entire cybersecurity profession dedicated to thwarting this behavior. Their main job is to protect the company from attacks from individuals who attempt to steal data, technologies, and intellectual property.

When we look at our marriages, we are in the business of providing safety and security as well. Both spouses always want to feel that they are protected and that they are in a safe and secure relationship. There are several behaviors that contribute to that sense of security – trust, honesty, transparency, loyalty, commitment, and fidelity.

It may not be immediately clear why trust falls under the safety and security umbrella, but a closer look reveals why. A spouse may feel completely secure if they believe without a shadow of a doubt that they have complete **trust** in their mate. With trust, there's an unspoken guarantee that there's someone there to come home to, to support you, and to build your life with. Without trust, the person may feel that this security could disappear at any moment, which could make it difficult to strengthen and maintain bonds within a marriage.

I would also put **honesty** in the same bucket. If I know that my spouse is always going to be open and honest with me, I feel a sense of security. I don't have to worry about whether my spouse's actions or words are being used to cover up their true feelings. There's an openness between us that reinforces our connection. I feel safe and secure knowing that my spouse will be honest with me.

Transparency is also key to providing greater security and safety. Not only is my spouse telling me the truth, but they're also revealing the motivations and reasoning behind what they're saying or doing. There's no tricky subtext or deceit. When there is transparency, your spouse does not have to read between the lines to uncover what you are not seeing or what you are not hearing.

It's also crucial to have a **secure home life**. This means that your home is a space where you can be your true self. Each person feels completely accepted for who they are – they don't have to pretend, maintain a façade, or wear a mask. They have the security and safety that their spouse loves them for who they really are.

This factors into feeling relaxed and comfortable in the relationship. Though there may be occasional moments of friction, but your relationship should be enjoyable overall. You look forward to spending time together, and when you do, it should feel natural. The conversation flows, the laughs keep coming, and neither person feels like every interaction takes work. Being together should not bring about any anxiety or stress; it's not something you run from. Instead, your relationship is your stress relief – it's where you retreat from the other parts of your life. It's your source of relaxation and comfort at all times.

Loving unconditionally can be tough for some people. However, in a safe and secure relationship, both individuals have a true belief that they will be loved unconditionally. There's security in knowing that the love they receive is not based on anything other than complete trust. When my father-in-law was asked how he and his wife of more than 60 years had stayed together for so long, he answered that they both understood that love was a choice. That they had committed to loving each other for better or for worse. That love was not just a feeling but a decision.

When you both have that complete understanding, you move through life with a sense of safety and security. You rest assured that your spouse will not walk out or give up on you because of a difficult situation. The safe and secure couple will choose to be with each other regardless of what happens.

Safety and security means my spouse will be there for me, regardless of the situation. I don't have to worry about who will have my back. Safety and security means no secrets. Secrets are ticking timebombs, and you want your spouse to know that you aren't withholding anything that could destroy your marriage.

There is safety and security in the fact that your spouse is a hard worker who does everything in his or her power to provide all of the resources that are needed for the family. Safety and security come from knowing that your spouse understands you and values who you are. And, safety and security come from knowing that you will not be judged on a daily basis. That you have a marriage that is judgment-free.

There is nothing more powerful than one spouse accepting the flaws of the other and not holding those flaws over their heads. We all have our flaws, and to know that those flaws won't be held against us, certainly reaffirms the strength of your bond.

Most of what has been described pertains to emotional safety and security. However, we cannot forget about **physical safety**. Safety of the home that you share together. Feeling safe when one of you are away from home. This is particularly true for the female spouse. She wants to know that her man is strong and has everything under control. She wants to feel physically safe when the two of them are together. Women want to know that their spouse will lay down their lives for them, that he is going to protect her and their family at all costs. She wants to feel assured that he is going to put her and the kids above himself.

There is **financial security** as well. This is addressed in more detail in another chapter. But there is safety and security in knowing that the finances are taken care of. This means the couple is not flooded with debt that can rob them of the safety and security they've worked so hard to build. Debt and improper management of money can make the couple feel like they are slaves to the bills and loans. There is nothing that contributes more to marital security than financial freedom.

There is security in knowing that you will be taken care of in the event something happens to your spouse, that plans are in place to provide for the spouse if the other dies. There is safety and security in knowing that those types of things are taken care of. The worst thing that can happen to a surviving spouse is for them to be left in financial ruin because proper steps were not taken to ensure every money matter was adequately handled.

PRINCIPLE #7

Having a Solid Financial Plan

You will not be surprised to know that businesses have a critical goal in mind. That goal is to be stable financially. Financial stability is critical to the overall success of any business. A great CEO of a business will ensure that the finances of the company are top priority each and every day. Having a sound financial platform allows the business to function and succeed in a wide variety of ways.

I have often heard that a steady stream of business is good but it is the management of finances and the resources that keep the business alive and well; this is also true for your marriage. The financial health of marriage is critical to its overall success.

Having disagreements and fights about money can really strain and do damage to the relationship. When couples are asked about the biggest issue that causes problems in their marriage, the number one answer is money. It is important for couples to understand how important this part of the marriage is for success. I am not saying that in order for the marriage to be successful there needs to be a certain amount of money coming into the household. I am saying how you handle and deal with the money you have coming in is what matters most.

Just like in business, you have to have a philosophy about money and how the money will be used to advance the business or the cause. Here are a few things to consider:

1. Have a plan or a budget that you both agree on:

Not having a plan or budget will allow for uncertainty and stress about how the money is being spent or if you will have enough to meet your needs. Be sure that part of your budget includes savings. The amount of money you have in your savings account determines your ability to respond to a financial crisis or emergency.

You need to have an emergency fund in case of a medical emergency or if one of you loses your job. Putting away money now, in preparation for a rainy day later, is smart financial planning. It's also smart to save money for the financial goals that you and your spouse have agreed upon, such as buying a house, buying a new car, taking family vacations and retirement. The two of you will need to decide how much money you will allocate and save monthly for each goal.

Dailyfinance.com recommends the 50/30/20 plan, where you allocate 20 percent of your monthly income for emergencies and save it in an emergency account. 50 percent is allocated for fixed expenses and the remaining 30 percent is for discretionary spending. If your financial situation won't allow you to follow this plan, then work with your spouse to develop a plan that's feasible for both of you.

2. *Communicate about your finances:*

Avoiding discussions about money will not make the money problems go away. Communication will be key to your success. This means discussing the sticky points that bring about stress and understanding your individual relationship with money(e.g. who is the spender and who is the saver?).

In essence, the core question is, "How do we get on the same page with our money?" Communicating will be instrumental in helping you to make big decisions that will have a significant impact on your finances. In short, talking about money will lead to better success.

Set a goal that you both agree on: What are your retirement goals? What major purchases will you need to make? There needs to be alignment with both partners on the long- and short-term goals for the finances.

3. Do not keep things hidden or keep secrets from your partner:

This is one of the biggest mistakes that married couples can make. Let's say the wife purchased a $200 pair of shoes and knows that the husband might not agree. It will be important for her to be open and honest and share that she made the purchase. Keeping it a secret will only make things worse in the long run, erode trust and possibly leave the couple's finances in a rough spot.

Both parties need to be as open and transparent as possible about their money. Remember, trust and transparency will be necessary in all departments of your marriage. But they're especially applicable here, and there should be full disclosure in all financial matters. This means no secret accounts, no hiding how much is in the savings or retirement accounts, and no purchasing of big-ticket items unless there is prior agreement (here, the two of you will have to decide what dollar amount constitutes a big-ticket item). When you have secret accounts, you lack transparency, and this will undermine your marriage and create layers of mistrust and dishonesty.

4. Don't be afraid to ask for help with the finances:

If it appears that you and your spouse are not making the progress that you need to make —seek help from a professional financial advisor. This will be money well spent to help secure your financial future.

5. Provide a financial update on a regular basis:

The couple should sit down with each other at least once a month to look over the finances, the budget and the goals. Can you imagine a company not reviewing their budget on a regular basis? Not keeping a close eye on the budget would more than likely put the business in jeopardy. The same holds true for the marriage.

You must set yourself up for success with knowledge. The best way to gain this knowledge is through information. This information will be generated each and every month, and it creates awareness for both partners about the state of their finances. It also allows you to do some course corrections if necessary.

6. Designate a CFO:

Giving your marriage the same respect that you give your business can have great benefits. In most business scenarios, there is a dedicated leader, but that person cannot run a successful business solo. Giving consideration to this fact, the Chief Financial Officer (CFO) seeks advice and relies on help from team members. Even if you are not the CFO, you are definitely part of the team, which gives you voting power to address, discuss and help implement the financial goals of the family.

Every successful business has a Chief Financial Officer who takes care of the financial matters of the company. Every successful marriage needs a CFO to address the financial needs of the family. More than likely, one of you is better at dealing with financial details like balancing the checkbook, paying the bills, and creating and maintaining a budget. After delegating a CFO, however, he or she doesn't get to make all the financial decisions. Remember, marriage is a "team effort" when it comes to decision making the two of you should set financial goals together. The CFO will have the responsibility of implementing what has been agreed upon.

Financial Management

'For richer or for poorer.' This is always said with lots of enthusiasm on the wedding day. Most couples are yet to understand what that particular line means; it is only seen as a routine recitation for wedding rites. After having a solid financial plan, there should be a discussion on financial management. Just like in business, both partners will have to discuss how to manage their finances, how much should be spent and how much should be saved. The shares, insurances, losses, profits, etc.? Bankruptcy could be the devastating result in business and in marriage when money is not well managed.

The steps below can help in managing your money effectively:

1. ***Clear your debts:*** If possible, clear all outstanding personal debts before tying the knot. Do not bring the burden of personal debt into marriage. This will help to avoid the financial implosion of both you and your partners money.

2. ***Write down your planned financial goals/Budget:*** It is very important for you and your partner to have financial goals. In other words, what would you like to accomplish with your money. After you have talked about your goals, create a budget. Write down how you are going to spend your money. Break things down into sections; rent, mortgage, school fees, food, vacations, retirement, etc. One good thing with the budget is that it guides your spending within your income and helps you to stay out of debt. Designing a

budget is not enough, you must also be disciplined to follow it and make adjustments when and where appropriate. Be sure to review for any incoming lapses. At the end of the day, will your budget allow you to accomplish the goals that you decide on?

3. ***Discuss bank accounts:*** How are you going to keep what you individually earn? Will it be a joint account or a separate account? Discuss this issue at length and make sure you are comfortable with your decision.

4. ***Set aside a contingency fund:*** This is the money for costs that are not within the budget. It is also called an "emergency fund" and would prevent both partners from suffering financial distress when unexpected issues arise. Contingency funds could solve unexpected problems such as job loss, relocation, illnesses, home repairs, etc. Contingency funds will always provide financial security for both partners.

5. ***Keep your credit card in check:*** Your credit card should not be used as an allowance to become extravagant. Credit cards are easy and tempting to use. If you do decide to use them, be sure to pay credit card charges monthly to avoid accumulating interest.

6. ***Save for retirement:*** Do not be caught financially off guard. Don't wait until you are retired before you start planning for it. Put in efforts to take advantage of any good retirement plans whether from your company or external sources.

7. ***Share responsibilities:*** Management of finances should not be the responsibility of one partner. Although one partner

can become the overseer or CFO of the finances, the overall management should involve both parties. Sharing of financial responsibilities helps to move the family forward if eventually, something happens to the other spouse. Each of the partners should share the responsibilities of managing the finances.

8. **A*cknowledge your spending habits:*** One partner might have a higher spending habit than the other. Acknowledge if you have excessive spending habits. It is recommended that you and your spouse talk about your spending habits and try to come up with a plan that is reasonable and acceptable to both of you.

9. ***Honesty:*** Never lie about your income. Some partners may lie about their income to avoid contributing as planned. Being honest is the best thing you could do for your partner when it comes to planning and managing finances. Also, when you purchase expensive items or spend money on a personal project, tell your spouse about it and be responsible for your actions.

10. ***Build trust:*** Trust your partner to handle financial responsibilities. Try not to watch their every step or constantly ask how money is being spent. You should have access to the family accounts and budget and if things are not adding up, you should ask your spouse about any financial discrepancies that you are seeing.

11. ***Stay out of debt:*** Try to stay out of debt. Debt can damage your financial plans and leave you in a difficult situation financially and emotionally.

Joint or Separate Accounts?

Keeping a joint or separate account can be a very difficult decision when managing your finances. Spouses may disagree on keeping joint accounts for lack of trust and the prospect of separation. There are pros and cons in regards to keeping joint or separate accounts. A joint account will allow both of you to view and manage your general household bills such as rent, mortgage, groceries, school costs, vacations, etc.

A joint account also ensures tracking spending habits since every expense needs to be recorded and explained. Also, a joint account ensures retaining of the finances without going through the rigorous process of the legal system if your spouse unfortunately passes away.

On the other hand, a joint account also has its own drawbacks. One of you may feel that you have lost of financial independence and resent having to explain every detail of your expenses.

There is also the possibility to decide to have seperate accounts. By having separate accounts you remove the expectation to constantly explain yourself for every transaction. In having a seperate account, you can agree how much to contribute into a joint account. This allows each partner to have some sense of financial independence. Partners can have both joint accounts and separate accounts, but there still needs to be accountability, transparency and honesty.

PRINCIPLE #8

Keeping Health and Wellness as High Priorities

My husband and I spent the majority of our early marriage just trying to build our family and our resources. We were working hard and not really taking a lot of time for ourselves. We were just living life as a busy married couple. We knew what we wanted out of life and out of our marriage. We wanted nice cars, a big house, a significant savings account, and the ability to travel when we wanted. We also wanted to be prepared for when we had kids. With all of that in mind, we worked hard and rarely took time for ourselves. We just focused on our incomes so we could fulfill the goals that we had outlined. Many of our goals pointed to material goods –our house, cars, and other miscellaneous purchases. It took us many years to realize that we were working hard but not taking the time to take care of ourselves. We were not focused at all on diet and exercise, or cognizant of how long hours at the office and limited hours of sleep were affecting our bodies. Nor did we realize the importance of taking time off or all of the elements that need to be in place to stay well and healthy. We finally decided that it was time for us to put things in perspective. We understood clearly that if we did not focus on our health, all of the material things would not mean anything. You cannot enjoy those things if you are struggling with your health. We made a commitment that we would focus more on our health and make it a major priority of our marriage. Once we decided to do that, and we implemented our health plan, we could tell that it made a significant difference in our happiness. We have been making health a priority ever since, and we have recommended this for many other couples. Some of the behaviors we adopted included signing up for gym memberships, working out several times a week, and cutting back on our consumption of processed foods and sugars.

Companies understand that the health of their employees is very important. Having healthy employees may boost company productivity, improve morale, help with the retention of current employees, attract other great employees, reduce the number of sick days used, improve engagement and possibly lower healthcare costs.

With married couples, the same may hold true. If we are in the best health, we will be more productive in our marriage, and our overall attitude toward our marriage and our spouse will be better. Being healthy will reduce the amount of time that we spend sick – which, in turn, reduces the amount of stress that we put on the marriage. If we are healthy, it may lead to better interactions between the married couple, and being healthy will also impact the finances - the less we are sick, the less days we'll miss at work and the less money we will spend on doctor's visits and medications.

Married couples need to invest time in taking good care of themselves. Being healthy is critically important to the overall success and happiness that couples will experience. If we are in the best health possible, it only makes us happier as individuals and as a married couple.

Additionally, many companies provide the opportunity for employees to take a certain number of days off during the year. They understand how important it is for employees to get away from the job to recharge themselves. They know that this leads to a happier employee.

Taking vacations is important for married couples as well. Taking the time to plan a vacation and travel is beneficial to the married couple in many different ways. First and foremost, it helps with the overall mental and psychological health of the couple.

Being away can bring about a feeling of calm and relaxation which, in turn, improves mental health. It also reduces stress and anxiety.

You and your spouse should make a plan to take vacations or short getaways each year. Getting away also ensures you have time that you can dedicate to each other. Recent studies show that couples who take the time to get away sleep better and are more positive overall.

Exercise is another important factor in the success of your marriage. You might wonder what exercise has to do with a successful marriage. However, there are so many benefits for those who exercise regularly, several of which have been touted for many, many years. The evidence is clear that people who exercise reduce their risk of many major diseases and disorders. There are so many studies that have validated this fact that it would be hard to dispute. So, regular exercise should be a major part of your marriage plan. The couple should pledge to each other that they will exercise and work on their overall health and wellness. For some married couples, exercising together has been an important component of their marriage. Some feel that exercising together is another opportunity for them to spend quality time together while also benefiting their health and wellness.

Healthy eating goes hand in hand with exercise. We have heard how critical it is to eat a healthy and balanced diet each and every day. Thus, making a pledge to each other to eat healthy is important. As a couple, you should sit down with each other and discuss what a healthy diet looks like for you individually and as a couple. You will have to understand what resonates with your partner in order for them to get on board with eating a healthy diet.

On the cautionary side, addictions are widespread in the workplace. I would venture to say that there are many individuals who are in marriages where one of the partners is involved in some type of addictive behavior. When the company realizes that there is an employee that is in trouble, they provide or find services for that individual. They will never just ask the person to leave. They work to provide services that will allow the individual to address the addictive behavior. The same holds true for our marriages. There may be times when one spouse will be addicted to a drug, alcohol or some other substance or activity. The other spouse must take the lead and be a supportive partner. This means taking steps to ensure your spouse gets the help they need. Leaving these types of issues unresolved will only lead to a much more difficult marriage.

Regular Visits to the Doctor

Men are notorious for not going to the doctor. Women are typically the opposite. Men will wait until something is terribly wrong before they go see a doctor. In most cases, men just don't rank health as a high priority. They tend to put it on the backburner. My husband had a good friend who loved beautiful vintage cars. He spent so much time washing and waxing these cars, always ensuring they were clean and in the best working condition. That meant that he put those cars at the top of his priority list. This same man was later diagnosed with late-stage cancer. He was hospitalized for several weeks and eventually passed away after the unsuccessful treatment of the cancer. Before he passed away, he shared with my husband that if he had to do it all over again, he would choose to put his time and energy into his own body and his own health instead of his cars. He was so busy with the cars that he put himself on the backburner. He told my husband that he had his priorities all screwed up. Regular visits to the doctor should've been a priority for him and they should be a priority for all of us.

Lower Health Care Costs

Being healthy will certainly lower you and your spouse's healthcare costs. In many cases, the company will pick up the tab for health care through its health insurance policy. However, these policies do not always cover every healthcare-related cost, meaning some visits, procedures, or medications need to be covered out-of-pocket. When both spouses are healthy, that requires less money to pay for health care services. We also know that health care costs are rising each and every year. The couple should strive hard to maintain a healthy lifestyle. Having a healthy lifestyle enables the couple to not only spend less time and money on medical needs but also remain happier about what is going on around them.

As a couple, you should sit down each year and review your health and wellness goals. You should also make sure you know where you are with regards to your overall health. If there are areas that you struggle with, you need to put them on the list for discussion. Making a pledge to each other that you will be as healthy as possible is important. If your goals do not line up, you will need to figure out a way to get on the same page.

PRINCIPLE #9

Evaluate and Then Evaluate Again

The strength of any company is based on how well they evaluate everything that they do. Assessments and evaluations are the cornerstone of companies getting better and better. It is so critical to evaluate services, products, and people in order to be the best company possible.

One critical aspect of most businesses is the employee evaluation period. This gives directors and managers the opportunity to evaluate their team members. There are sets of measures that they use to determine how well employees are doing. Some of the more common evaluation measures include overall knowledge of the job, quality of overall work, attendance and punctuality, the amount of initiative the employee takes, their communication and listening skills, and how dependable they are.

Employees are scored in each of these areas. Once they are scored, the supervisor will meet with the employee and walk through each measure and provide the score with examples of why they were scored high or low. It is important to not just focus on what is going wrong but also give feedback on the things that are going well.

When you think about your marriage, the same type of scenarios should serve as a reference. Every marriage needs to be evaluated at some point in time. This allows you to take a step back and look at the overall condition of your relationship and all aspects of your union. By taking this step back, it gives both of you the opportunity to see what you are doing well and what areas need improvement. Where do you need to grow as individuals and where do you need to grow as a married couple?

Many couples that I have talked to never think about setting aside time to evaluate their marriage. They often go year after year with the same issues and problems with no plan in place to address them. There is no plan because the problems have not been clearly identified. The couple should be having an ongoing conversation about what is going well and what is not. There are things that can be addressed immediately and there are things that may require more time.

It is suggested that the married couple compile a list of things that they agree should be evaluated, such as:

- How would you assess our love life?

- How can I be a better husband/wife?

- What behaviors or activities would you like to see me doing more often?

- Do we compliment each other enough?

- What should I stop doing immediately?

- How is our financial situation? Are we following our budget?

- How effectively are we communicating?

- Do you feel supported?

- What can I do better to show you how much I love you?

- Are we satisfied with our spiritual life?

- How are we doing in the child-rearing/family planning category?

- Are there areas of trust that we need to work on?

- What do you need from me that I am not giving?

- Are we taking good care of our health and wellness?
- Do we fight and argue fairly?
- Do we feel that we are engaging each other enough?
- How do we feel about the time that we spend together?
- Do you have any issues with my appearance?
- How would we evaluate our overall home life?
- Do we have full control over our social media habits?
- Do we feel good about our work situations?
- Do we do a good job of making shared decisions?
- Do we take care of the house the way we should?
- Do we take enough time off?

This is not an exhaustive list but some things to consider. I want to emphasize that you want to talk about things that are going well in addition to those things that are not. There is often a tendency to talk about what's going wrong without acknowledging the positives.

For those areas where some additional work is needed, the married couple will need to put a plan in place to make it better. The plan needs to be very specific, with actions that can be measured by each. For example, if a spouse was concerned about spending more time together, the plan might include a goal of going on a date with each other at least once a week. That is a measurable and specific goal. For each area of improvement, there should be a clear way to measure success over time. Bringing up significant issues that cannot be measured might prove difficult to assess during the next evaluation period. The couple needs to be as specific as possible in order to get the most out of this important work.

My husband and I started doing this evaluation about 15 years after we were married. We were not very intentional about sitting down and talking about things that were going well and those things that were not. We would just go through the motions. Periodically, one of us might complain about something in our marriage. We would talk about it and the other spouse would agree to try to do better. But there would be no concrete plan of action. We just took each other's word that we would take the necessary steps to get better.

We finally decided that we needed to be more intentional about communicating the good and the bad. We began *treating our marriage like a business*. We talked about areas that were important to us. We discussed how we were doing in each area and walked away with a plan to address the weaknesses. This worked very well for us as our marriage matured. We both had a clear line of sight to those areas that needed our full attention. We also had specific measurable behaviors that kept us moving in the right direction. If we saw that we were moving off track, we could make an immediate course correction.

The other thing that we started doing, which we cannot take credit for, is going on a yearly marriage retreat. We have friends that have been doing this for years. It is the opportunity to get away from the normal day-to-day duties of marriage and take some focused time together to talk about all aspects of the union. There is a misperception that a marriage retreat is all about intimacy and lovemaking.

A true marriage retreat includes those areas but, more importantly, it is also an opportunity for open and honest dialogue about the successes and challenges of the marriage. It's a productive time in an isolated location where a couple can discuss critical items and walk away with a plan to address the problems while also reinforcing the good things.

Both spouses should take some time prior to leaving for the retreat to prepare their discussion points. Everything is fair game for the retreat agenda.

The most important thing is for the communication to be completely open and honest – no beating around the bush, no sugar coating, no avoidance. Pure, unadulterated truth is the only way that things will get better. At the end of the retreat, you should have a document that outlines everything that was discussed and the resolution for each point on the agenda. This document will be the guiding light for the next year. It is recommended that the document is reviewed at least once a month to keep it fresh on the minds of both spouses.

The other key aspect of employee evaluation is setting the goals for the next year. I think this is important in a marriage as well. Setting goals for what you want to accomplish in the upcoming year, within the next five years, etc, is advantageous for the couple. A goal could be that you want to keep learning about how to strengthen the marriage. Or, you could make a goal to go back to school and get an additional degree. Remember to make sure all your goals are clear, specific, and actionable.

Conducting a SWOT Analysis

A very common tool that is used in business is the SWOT analysis. It is a strategic planning tool that helps companies or individuals identify the strengths, weaknesses, opportunities, and threats related to making the business more competitive or successful. The SWOT analysis takes a hard look at the internal and external factors that can positively or negatively affect a company or individual's ability to achieve their stated goals and objectives.

Strengths are the characteristics of the company or business that give it an advantage over the competition.

Weaknesses are the characteristics of that company or business that put it at a disadvantage compared to others.

Opportunities are those characteristics that the company can use as an advantage to increase their strengths.

Threats are those characteristics that could cause issues or problems that slow or block the success of the business.

This is a great tool to use as part of the evaluation and assessment of your marriage. In most cases for businesses, this tool is used during a strategic planning session. I think using this to do an overall assessment of your marriage works well. If we think about it, each marriage has these same elements to consider. What are the strengths, weaknesses, opportunities, and threats of your marriage?

Strengths - There are certain things in your marriage that you would consider strengths. These are things that are going well that both you and your spouse are very happy with. Take some time to sit with your spouse and talk about those things that you feel are strengths. For example, is your marriage strong in the area of communication? Do you feel good about the amount of time you spend together? Are your finances exactly where you want them to be? Are both of you being sexually satisfied?

Weaknesses - These are the areas of your marriage that you feel can use some significant improvements. This will probably be the most difficult conversation you will have with the SWOT analysis. This is where transparent conversations need to take place. If you do not openly communicate the weaknesses, your marriage will not have those targets of improvement. This is not the time to argue or fight about what one sees as weaknesses; this is the time to just listen. For example, if the wife does not feel that she is being satisfied in the bedroom, the husband just needs to listen to her and have a conversation about how to improve in that area. You must try not to take everything personally at this point. Your spouse is only identifying those things that can make your marriage stronger. If the husband identifies the fact that the wife is not taking good care of herself and continues to put on weight, the woman just needs to listen to him and think about and discuss ways that she can do better in this area.

Opportunities - These are those things that you might be able to control in your environment. These may be more external factors that can help the marriage. These are things like hiring a housekeeper that will take some of the burden off of the wife for taking care of the house. If the husband's job is causing him significant stress and anxiety that spills over into the marriage, he may consider finding a new job. If health is an issue, the couple may consider joining a fitness center or committing to working out together three times a week. It may be a good idea to focus on opportunities that can impact either strengths or weaknesses.

Threats- This part of the analysis can also be difficult to discuss. It will depend significantly on how strong and stable the marriage currently is. The threats are those areas that can literally bring down the marriage, those items that might lead a spouse to walk away from the marriage. For example, is the man showing signs and signals that he is having an affair? Does the wife have a flirting relationship with a male coworker? Is social media taking control of either spouse's time? Does the couple feel that they are not satisfying each other in the bedroom? Is the couple close to being in financial ruin? Are the bills and financial responsibilities too much for them to overcome? These are certainly major threats but don't feel pressured to identify only major issues. There could also be minor threats with the potential to cause a major disruption in the marriage over time.

One appearingly minor threat that we are seeing more and more of today is social media. Having a Facebook or Instagram page could be innocent enough, but it can become overwhelming to some people. There are couples who struggle significantly because of the amount of time they spend on social media. There are also examples of men and women reconnecting with their old high school sweethearts or exes through their accounts. In these cases, a seemingly minor threat could turn into a major one.

It Can Only Get Better

In every business, there is always hope for growth. No matter the accruing losses, there is always a positive side for improvement. If all businesses focused on their losses then there would be no businesses around. This holds for marriage as well; if you keep holding onto the flaws of your partner, having negative attitudes towards your marriage, nothing will ever work out. Find ways to improve yourself and become better for your partner; build a healthy communication pattern with your partner, trust your partner completely, be positive, do not rush into making decisions, say words of encouragement to your partner, cultivate a healthy sexual life and enjoy each other's company.

This should be your hope always - it can only get better.

PRINCIPLE #10

Understanding and Living Our Culture and Values

Many organizations have values that guide how they think about things and how they conduct business. For example, a company may have a list of values that include things like integrity, trust, accountability, passion, diversity, innovation, and teamwork. Companies have these values because they help guide their decision making and point of view for every aspect of the business. These values also send a message to team members and their customers about what the organization stands for, and they help job seekers understand more about the company they may work for.

In marriage, the same holds true. There needs to be a set of guiding values or principles that the husband and wife mutually agree upon that keep them on the same page. The values that I believe are important to the marriage can be found in the word of God, the Bible. God has set standards and values that married couples should adhere to.

God established the institution/covenant of marriage when He created Adam and Eve, thus taking a rib from Adam's side and creating a woman for Adam whom he named Eve. Adam and Eve were the first married couple, the first true example of husband and wife. The Bible teaches us that God established marriage for the good of all mankind. It's a permanent partnership of life and love. I believe that the spiritual aspect of marriage is the nucleus that helps determine the health and success of every marriage. God created man and woman in His own image, so acknowledging God and being in fellowship with God will help to develop and maintain a healthy, thriving marriage. This should be considered the core value of the marriage.

Marriage is more than a physical union; it's also a spiritual and emotional one. Thus, there are many important values to have in your marriage. I have identified six that I think are absolutely necessary. These values are based on the essential belief that the culture of your marriage is based on your relationship with God.

Unconditional Love

Of all the values, I feel that love is the most important. Unconditional love means loving without limitations or conditions. It is love that cannot be earned but is given freely. **1 Corinthians 13:4-5 (NIV)** tells us that "Love is patient, love is kind. It does not envy, it does not boast, it is not proud. It does not dishonor others, it is not self-seeking, it is not easily angered, it keeps no record of wrongs." This particular scripture is the foundation for your marital relationship. It is the blueprint that shows us how we should communicate and interact with each other as husband and wife. We should not be prideful or boastful. We should be patient and kind towards each other. We should not hold grudges; we should be slow to anger and easy to forgive. We should not keep records of each other's mistakes or keep a score of wrongdoings. We should love each other freely and unconditionally just as our Heavenly Father loves us.

Another one of my favorite "love" scriptures is **Ephesians 5:25-31 NIV**: "Husbands, love your wives, just as Christ also loved the church and gave Himself for her, that He might sanctify and cleanse her with the washing of water by the word, that He might present her to Himself a glorious church, not having spot or wrinkle or any such thing, but that she should be holy and without blemish. So husbands ought to love their own wives as their own bodies; he who loves his wife loves himself. For no one ever hated his own flesh, but nourishes and cherishes it, just as the Lord does the church. For we are members of His body, of His flesh and of His bones. For this reason a man shall leave his father and mother and be joined to his wife, and the two should become one flesh.

This scripture describes the parallel between Christ and the church being one body and the husband and wife being one flesh. Whatever the husband does to his wife, he does it unto himself also. Marriage is a metaphor for the relationship between Christ and the church. So, the husband does not have automatic control over his wife just because he is the husband. Rather he has the responsibility to love like Christ, freely and unconditionally.

There are a few other favorite scriptures that stress the importance of love:

Colossians 3:14(NIV): "And over all these virtues put on love, which binds them all together in perfect unity."

1 Corinthians 16:14(NIV): "Do everything in love."

1 Peter 4:8 (NIV): "Above all, love each other deeply, because love covers over a multitude of sins."

John 15:12 (NIV): "My command is this: Love each other as I have loved you."

1 Corinthians 13:13 (NIV): "And now these three remain: faith, hope, and love. But the greatest of these is love."

Faithfulness

Being faithful is very important to the success and stability of marriage. Someone who is faithful has a firm and constant devotion to someone or something, usually by means of an oath or pledge. For married couples, it's their wedding vows. Being faithful not only means that you are not having sex with other people, but it also means that your romantic and intimate feelings should be reserved and directed toward your spouse only. **Proverbs 3:3-4 (NIV):** "Let love and faithfulness never leave you; bind them around your neck, write them on the tablet of your heart. Then you will win favor and a good name in the sight of God and man." This scripture in Proverbs lets us know how important faithfulness is. It is so important that we are instructed to bind love and faithfulness around our neck and write them on the tablet of our hearts. By doing so, we will have a constant reminder to love our spouse unconditionally and remain faithful at all times.

"No temptation has overtaken you except such as is common to man; but God *is* faithful, who will not allow you to be tempted beyond what you are able, but with the temptation will also make the way of escape, that you may be able to bear it."**1 Corinthians 10:13 (NKJV).** This scripture informs us that temptation is common to man. A strong prayer life and strategic planning should help you overcome temptation and remain faithful. A few strategies that can help are below:

Accept the fact that you are no longer single. You are an individual and you should still plan and enjoy "alone time" as well as time and activities with your spouse. But too much alone time may not be good for the relationship.

Plan frequent activities together and schedule routine and quality time together so the two of you can unwind, stay connected and enjoy each other.

Invest in your marriage. Make it a priority and do things to continually work on you and your relationship. This could include date nights, marriage retreats, marriage coaching or counseling as well as individual coaching or counseling.

Maintain and enjoy an active sex life. I know we all think that sex should be spontaneous but after long days at work and evenings filled with events, kids and the demands and routines of home life, sometimes sex can be placed at the bottom of the list. If this is the case, plan a time to have sex. That's right – put it on your calendar or make a mental note of it. You'll see, it will be just as satisfying and planned sex is better than no sex at all.

This next one is a big one for me and I stress it in my relationship coaching all the time. Maintain appropriate barriers and boundaries. I could write a book on this alone. But for the sake of time, I will only list a few examples. If you are having marital problems, don't discuss them with someone of the opposite sex. Refrain from flirting- there is no such thing as innocent flirting. Hang out with other married couples. Join a marital group. Find someone who has been successfully married for many years and ask them to mentor you and your spouse. Keep God first and centered in your relationship and agree that quitting is not an option.

Exodus 20:14 (NIV) says that you shall not commit adultery. This is a core value that both individuals must adhere to. The husband and the wife must agree that this is a value that they will always honor. Committing adultery will absolutely devastate a marriage. That is one thing that can undo a marriage very quickly. It is not to say that one cannot forgive a spouse who committed adultery. But you do not want to put yourself in a position of having to address it in the first place.

Peace

Peace has been defined as being tranquil or calm; a state or period in which there is no war. As married couples are in the routine of their daily lives, and experiencing all of the emotional and physical challenges that they encounter during the rotation (i.e. work, marriage – which is work, kids, illness, etc.), conflict and stress are bound to creep in. And when conflict is mishandled, or daily stressors go unaddressed, you can create an environment where there is an absence of peace. "Be completely humble and gentle; be patient, bearing with one another in love. Make every effort to keep the unity of the Spirit through the bond of peace." **Ephesians 4:2-3 (NIV)**

Peace is attainable and maintainable. I would like to suggest ten ways to seek and maintain peace in your marriage:

- Try to maintain a peaceful state of mind.
- Identify triggers and try to stay away from people and situations that rob you of your peace.
- Keep the lines of communication open.
- Speak the truth in love.
- Listen before you speak.
- You don't have to say everything you think.
- Avoid accusing, judging or pointing the finger.
- Be slow to take offense and be easy to forgive.
- Be responsible and accountable for your own actions.
- Remember your spouse is not the enemy.
- Pray together daily.

Forgiveness

Forgiveness is a choice. Often, it's not an easy choice to make but when you choose to forgive, God will release you from your prison of anger, bitterness, pain, torment, and resentment.

The ability to request forgiveness and give it is one of the most important factors of marital happiness. Make allowances for each other's faults and make an effort to always forgive.

Forgiveness can very well be your key to happiness. Forgiveness doesn't give you or your spouse free reign to make poor decisions, but it sets you free. When you choose to forgive, you are setting two people free; one is the person you have forgiven and the other one is you!

If you feel you have offended your spouse or they have indicated you offended them, go to them and ask them to help you understand the offense. After you understand the offense, admit that you are wrong and apologize. Ask for their forgiveness. If your spouse does not immediately forgive you, then wait for it. While you wait, stay in love. Be sure to give your spouse the space that he or she needs. While waiting, pray that God will help enlighten you about how to better communicate with your spouse.

Building Spiritual Intimacy In Your Marriage

Spiritual intimacy is learning how to connect with your spouse through your faith. Building spiritual intimacy is the shared responsibility of both partners as both come together and surrender their lives to Christ. Despite the roadblocks to building a spiritual culture, every relationship that has experienced the power of spiritual intimacy has a connection that always keeps them together.

Spiritual intimacy benefits a relationship by:

- Creating a deeper level of love between partners.
- Experience God's love at a more intimate level.
- Increase the odds of a successful marriage.
- Opens the door to a deeper understanding of each other.
- Reveals God's purpose and plans for your lives.

You can grow your spiritual intimacy by:

- Praying together: Never let a day pass without praying with your partner.
- Study the word of God together: Schedule times to study and share the word together. Encourage each other.
- Spend time with other mature Christian couples.
- Live out the purpose of God in your lives. Pass on your faith to those around you.
- Show gratitude to God and count your blessings.

Striving to grow spiritually and working towards spiritual intimacy can be one of the best gifts you could give your partner and your marriage.

Intimacy

Song of Solomon 4:9 (NIV): "You have stolen my heart, my sister, my bride; you have stolen my heart with one glance of your eyes, with one jewel of your necklace."

We should look at sex as a gift from God. This gift allows us as a married couple to experience the most intense, profound and deepest intimacy. Intimacy includes more than our sexual relationship. The intimacy in our marriages should be growing daily. We should have dedicated time to talk to each other and to spend time alone with each other. We should also make a habit of praying together and seek God's guidance in the continual development and growth of our relationship.

Unity

Ecclesiastes 4:9-12 (NIV): "Two are better than one, because they have a good return for their labor: If either of them falls down, one can help the other up. But pity anyone who falls and has no one to help them up. Also, if two lie down together, they will keep warm. But how can one keep warm alone? Though one may be overpowered, two can defend themselves. A cord of three strands is not quickly broken."

Marriage is a covenant. It is a relationship between two people who have agreed to be open and honest with each other and who have made a commitment to be faithful to one another and work through the highs and the lows of the relationship. As a couple, you should be mindful of your words and be cognizant of your spouse's feelings and emotions. Remind your partner often of how much you appreciate them and be sure to say "thank you" for the little things that they do. Be mindful of your appearance and compliment your spouse on a regular basis. Take note of the time and energy that they put into looking nice and be sure that you recognize their efforts. Be the first one to apologize or say, "I'm sorry". You will be surprised how much this little action will help to improve the airways of communication. Work on any jealous behavior that either of you have and do things that will improve your sense of security. Involve yourselves in independent activities that interest you and remember to make time to enjoy things that you have in common. Work on having a strong prayer life. Praying together will strengthen your intimate connection and your relationship with God. And last but not least, remember that your marriage is your number one priority. Respect and value your marriage and watch your union grow.

PRINCIPLE #11

No Business Allowed

When every part of your day has been dedicated to phone calls, meetings, supervising schedules, interacting with colleagues and adhering to to-do lists, you need a place where you can enjoy the total opposite of all that you have engaged in during your day.

In all other areas of this book, I have talked about the benefits that you accrue or experience by treating your marriage like you treat your business; giving your marriage the same respect that you give your business or job; putting in at least the same amount of hours (preferably more), and attending to or addressing the needs of your marriage just like you would attend to or address the needs of your business. But there is one area of your marriage, one room in your house, where I will recommend that NO business transactions take place – the bedroom.

Each room in your house is designed for certain activities and events to take place. The kitchen was built so you can have your nutritional needs met. The living room was designed for relaxation. The den was designed for fun and fellowship. And the bedroom is designed for ......shhh! Seriously, your bedroom was designed for you and your spouse to have a place to have quiet time, relaxation, rest and reconnection. And due to the fact that the bedroom's purposeful design is so totally different from what the other rooms in your house were designed for, the bedroom should inherently have a different set of rules. The No.1 Rule: No Business Allowed!!!

You should consider your bedroom a sanctuary, a daily getaway, a retreat. Your bedroom should be a special place for you and your spouse. I know couples whose bedrooms become the cartoon lounge on Saturday mornings for them and their kids, or it becomes the place where teens can sneak away to have private phone conversations or to get a break from their younger siblings. I strongly recommend the bedroom not being used for anything other than sleep and intimacy for couples. I am definitely an advocate for family fun and gatherings in and around the home, but just not in mom and dad's bedroom. I think when the parents' bedroom becomes just another routine gathering or meeting place in the house, it loses some of its aura of being a sanctuary for them to retreat or reconnect after they have had a long and strenuous day.

A lot of couples do make the mistake of conducting business in the bedroom. They use the bedroom as a carryover space from the workday to finish emails, respond to text messages, check out the latest stories on the news, or get their daily dose of social media. They use the bedroom as a place to continue disagreements or plan the latest intervention for their children. I think you see where I'm going with this. Anything that is going to overload the mind or set the mood for contention should not be entertained in the bedroom. Though I know there are likely many of you who will argue that reading a book in bed or watching a movie relaxes you and helps you go to sleep.

Conducting business in the bedroom can be an aphrodisiac killer. Do your best to leave anything that's heavy or negative at the door and when you enter your bedroom; be prepared to indulge in things that bring you happiness and joy. You may want to talk with your spouse about your day but be careful that it won't destroy the mood for intimacy and relaxation. What if you are not in the mood for talking or for sex? Entering into your sanctuary or retreat for nothing more than a good night's sleep is not only permissible, it's profitable. Sleep deprivation affects your mood, your behavior, your communication and your performance at work. So, when you haven't had enough sleep, not only does it have a negative impact on you, but it also negatively affects those around you. A good night's sleep is beneficial to you and inadvertently to those who are close to you.

Whether you know it or not, your environment affects your mood. The way your space is organized, the furniture, the decor, the way it looks, the way it smells, all have a profound effect on the way you respond to or interact with your surroundings. Since we typically start and end our day in one room, we want to be cognizant of the energy that we receive from that room. So, sprucing up your bedroom, changing the color scheme, dimming the lights, adding candles, and making it cozier will help to ensure that your bedroom is restricted from business and open for romance, rest and relaxation.

The Beauty of Sex

Sex is not all about the physical coming together of both partners. It is deeper than just a physical act. Sex in marriage should not be exclusively the act of lovemaking, there should also be a deep feeling of intimacy. The bedroom should be a sanctuary for the overall growth of each partner, a place for knowing each other and fulfilling your needs. Here are a few ways to heighten your sexual experience;

1. Be vulnerable: What do you have to hide in the bedroom? No pretense, everything is uncovered and laid bare. Let your guard down and be bare, enjoy the process and never hold back.

2. Be passionate: You have to let go of every distraction. Have you ever been passionate about anything? This is the time to be passionate, allow yourself to be carried away in the process.

3. Do not be too serious: It is not actually a battle. Lovemaking should be playful and interesting. You can laugh and be joyful in the moment.

4. Allow yourself to transcend beyond the physical: One thing is for sure; sex cannot be removed from the activities of marriage. So you have to enjoy the moments and the mind-blowing orgasms it presents. This is what God wants for you as a married couple - to enjoy the sacredness of sex.

Sex is paramount in every marriage and this has made the bedroom the center of every relationship. It is where many extraordinary things happen.

CONCLUSION

I am writing this book from years of personal experience and the experiences of those who I have counseled. I have been married for almost 33 years. My husband and I have used many of these business principles successfully. I am certain that the reason we have had a successful marriage is because we implemented most of these principles and because of our relationship with God. The unfortunate part is that we did not discover these principles on day one. It took us a while to figure this out. I am sharing this because I would like for those newly married couples to get this concept early. This will certainly allow you the opportunity to avoid some of the pitfalls that my husband and I and a lot of other couples have experienced. It is also for those who have been married for many years. Like the old saying goes, "It is never too late."

A multi-million dollar business owner was asked during his marriage Golden Jubilee (50 years)? "How did you do it?" and he replied," I treat my marriage the way I treat my business". The truth is the business approach to marriage might not be viewed as romantic and therefore may not capture the interest of some couples. You had imagined a blissful union with your partner where everything look perfect. As life happens, things begin to look less perfect and more practical. And when things begin to fall apart, you need a plan in place to restore the marriage. No business owner would want their business to fail; they would go against all odds to put every strategy in place to save their business. The same should be true for married couples.

The positive effects of a business approach to your marriage would be visible in your; decision making, marriage plans, your ability to have proper knowledge of your spouse, your pattern of communication with your partner, time management, financial planning, and your spirituality. However, the key to a successful marriage is not a 'one size-fits-all'. No two marriages are the same, find your best fit and the business principles that work for you, and live your best life with your partner.

www.ingramcontent.com/pod-product-compliance
Lightning Source LLC
Chambersburg PA
CBHW030328080526
44584CB00012B/770